AN ILLUSTRATED GUIDE TO

The Lost Symbol

EDITED BY JOHN WEBER

CONTRIBUTING EDITORS
PATRICK HUYGHE & MICHAEL BOBER

POCKET BOOKS

New York   Toronto   Sydney   London

The editor has made every reasonable effort to identify the owners of the rights to the content of this book and obtain their permission to include it. If you believe you are the owner of the rights of any content in this book but were not contacted by the editor, he apologizes and will correct his mistake in subsequent editions. Please write to the editor c/o Sensei Publications LLC, 217 Thompson Street #473, New York, NY 10012.

 Pocket Books
A Division of Simon & Schuster, Inc.
1230 Avenue of the Americas
New York, NY 10020

First Pocket Books trade paperback edition November 2009

POCKET and colophon are registered trademarks of Simon & Schuster, Inc.

Full credits, copyright, and permissions information can be found on page 180; which is an extension of this copyright page.

For information about special discounts for bulk purchases, please contact Simon & Schuster Special Sales at 1-866-506-1949 or business@simonandschuster.com

The Simon & Schuster Speakers Bureau can bring authors to your live event.
For more information or to book an event contact the Simon & Schuster Speakers Bureau at 1-866-248-3049 or visit our website at www.simonspeakers.com.

Design and production by Laura Smyth, Smythtype Design.

Manufactured in the United States of America

10 9 8 7 6 5 4 3 2 1

Library of Congress Cataloging-in-Publication Data is available from the publisher.

ISBN 978-1-4165-2366-6
ISBN 978-1-4391-8065-5 (ebook)

CONTENTS

(Locations in *The Lost Symbol* are in red)

FINDING THE LOST SYMBOLS IN WASHINGTON, D.C.

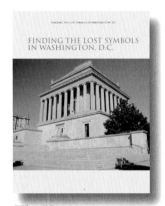

The House of the Temple 1

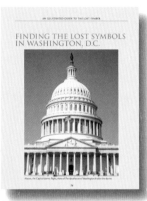

The Capitol 54

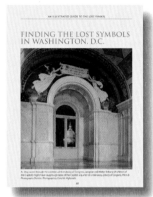

The Library of Congress 88

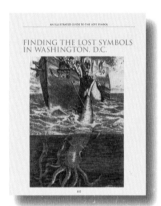

The Smithsonian Museum Support Center 112

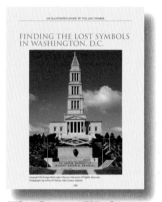

The George Washington Masonic Memorial 136

Kryptos 154

The Washington Monument 170

A Note from the Editor

I n *The Lost Symbol* (as in *The Da Vinci Code* and *Angels & Demons*), Robert Langdon sees and deciphers the secret meaning of symbols embedded in art and architecture. The reader only "sees" these symbols in his or her imagination.

Since the Langdon novels are based on fact, this art and architecture actually exist, and no matter how vivid your imagination is, you'd be hard-pressed to imagine the Temple Room in the House of the Temple, or *The Apotheosis of Washington*, or the statue of Washington as Zeus. The George Washington Masonic Memorial and *Kryptos* defy imagination! So the first function of our book (and I say "our" because over eighty people have been involved in the creation of this book) is to take you to these places and let you see what they look like with your own eyes. The "Finding the Lost Symbols in Washington, D.C." chapters follow the action of *The Lost Symbol* and feature the locations central to the story.

The second function of our book is to fill in some of the history Dan Brown can only allude to in a novel. The numbered chapters elaborate on the origin and history of Freemasonry, the role of Freemasons in the founding of the United States and the design and building of Washington, D.C. Also presented are some of the treasures on display in the Capitol Building and Library of Congress. And finally, we have a primer on Noetic Science from Edgar Mitchell, who started the Institute of Noetic Science—to Marilyn Schlitz (a likely model for the Katherine Solomon character) to Dean Radin, Senior Scientist at IONS.

Heartfelt thanks to Patrick Huyghe and Michael Bober on the editorial side; Laura Smyth for her brilliant design; Louise Burke and Anthony Ziccardi of Simon & Schuster and Sandra Martin and Alexander Dake at Paraview for making this book possible.

John Weber
Brooklyn, NY 2009

FINDING THE LOST SYMBOLS IN WASHINGTON, D.C.

The House of the Temple

Dan Brown opens *The Lost Symbol* in the Temple Room of the House of the Temple, with Dr. Christopher Abaddon being raised to a 33rd-degree Mason, and returns there for its denouement.

Located at 1733 Sixteenth Street, N.W. (Sixteenth Street is referred to as "The Corridor of Light" by Masons), the House of the Temple is headquarters for the Supreme Council (Mother Council of the World) of the Inspectors General Knights Commander of the House of the Temple of Solomon of the Thirty-third Degree of the Ancient and Accepted Scottish Rite of Freemasonry of the Southern Jurisdiction of the United States of America. (Yes, there is also a Northern Jurisdiction, which has its headquarters at the National Heritage Museum in Lexington, Massachusetts.)

Visitors (both Masons and non-Masons) are welcome and tours are conducted on the hour or half hour. The hours of operation are in flux owing to the Dan Brown effect, so it's best to call before visiting: (202) 232-3579. Photography is permitted—and encouraged.

The name "House of the Temple" refers to the Temple of Solomon, the building that is central to Masonic ritual and symbolism.

The cornerstone for the House of the Temple was laid in 1911 and the building was completed in 1915. It is modeled after the Mausoleum of Halicarnasses, one of the original Seven Wonders of the World.

Sphinx, eyes open.

Sphinx, eyes closed.

Above: Unfinished pyramid roof of the House of the Temple. Below: Temple entrance.

John Russell Pope was the architect for the House of the Temple. He subsequently designed the Jefferson Memorial, the National Archives, and the National Gallery of Art.

A visitor must pass between two massive sphinxes to enter the front door, one with its eyes open (perhaps representing thought, perception or engagement with the outer world) and one with its eyes closed (perhaps suggesting meditation, contemplation or "soul-building"). Thirty-three columns—each thirty-three feet high—surround the building. And there are thirty-three seats in the Temple Room.

The roof of the House of the Temple is an "unfinished" pyramid, consisting of thirteen steps.

Although difficult to see from the street, visitors to Washington, D.C., can view this pyramid "floating in the air" looking south from Meridian Hill Park—in the foreground of the Washington Monument.

The First Inauguration of George Washington, April 30, 1787   *by John D. Melius*

Photo by Maxwell Mackenzie

George Washington's Inauguration as the 1st President of the United States, Apr. 30, 1789

This painting and its companion, George Washington Laying the Cornerstone of the United States Capitol, September 18, 1793, *both reside in the George Washington Memorial Banquet Hall of the House of the Temple.*

The building in the background is Federal Hall, in New York City. After swearing the oath of office, President Washington famously kissed the Holy Bible, which was on loan from the St. John's Lodge, also located in New York.

The historical figures participating in the ceremony include quite a few prominent Freemasons. The twelve men depicted are, left to right:

1. Frederick William von Steuben, a Mason, was an army officer and aide-de-camp to Frederick the Great of Prussia. Von Steuben became a Major General during the Revolution and was known as the "drill master of the Continental Army."

2. **John Jay,** right and in the foreground, then Secretary of State, later became a Supreme Court Justice.

3. **John Adams** was the first Vice President and became the second President of the United States.

4. **Henry Lee,** a Mason, was known as "Light Horse Harry Lee" because of his brilliant cavalry operations in the Revolutionary War. He was also the father of General Robert E. Lee.

5. **Robert R. Livingston,** a Mason, was Chancellor of the State of New York and Grand Master of New York Masons from 1784 to 1800. He is to Lee's right, by the railing.

6. **Samuel Otis,** Secretary of the Senate, holds the Bible from St. John's Lodge No. 1, New York City.

7. **George Washington,** a Mason, stands with his right hand placed on the Bible.

8. **Morgan Lewis,** a Mason, was Grand Marshall during this ceremony and later became a Major General in the War of 1812. He was elected Grand Master of New York Masons in 1830.

9. **Frederick A. C. Muhlenberg,** a Mason, appears in a gold-colored coat. Born in Pennsylvania, he was educated in Germany as a Lutheran clergyman and was the elected Speaker of the House of Representatives.

10. **Arthur St. Clair,** a Mason, is dressed in military uniform. He was born in Scotland and came to America with the British Army in 1757 only to become a Major General in the Continental Army. At the time of the inauguration, he was the Governor of the Northwest Territory.

11. **George Clinton,** next to St. Clair, was Governor of New York at the time of the inauguration.

12. **Henry Knox,** a Mason, was a close adviser to Washington and a Major General and Chief of Artillery in the Revolutionary Army. He is to the far right in the painting and was Secretary of War at the time of Washington's first inauguration.

The Temple Room

Right: The Oculus.
Below: Interior view of the Temple Room.
Photo by Maxwell Mackenzie

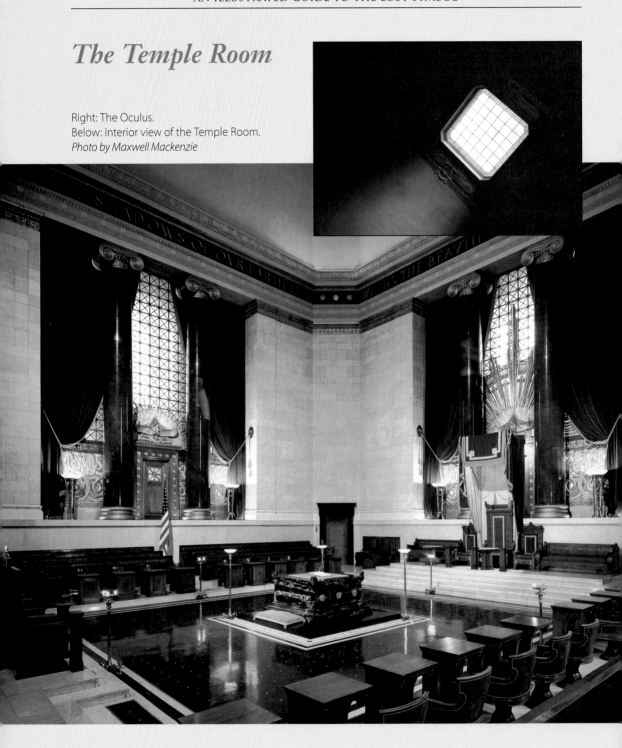

CHAPTER ONE
Freemasonry and the Ancient Mysteries

"The origin of Freemasonry is one of the
most debated, and debatable, subjects
in the whole realm of historical enquiry."

—Frances A. Yates

The Mysteries   *by W. L. Wilmshurst*

W. L. Wilmshurst is the author of The Meaning of Masonry, *from which this is excerpted.*

In all the periods of the world's history, and in every part of the globe, secret orders and societies have existed outside the limits of the official churches for the purpose of teaching what are called "the Mysteries": for imparting to suitable and prepared minds certain truths of human life, certain instructions about divine things, about the things that belong to our peace, about human nature and human destiny, which it would be undesirable to publish to the multitude who would but profane those teachings and apply the esoteric knowledge that was communicated to perverse and perhaps to disastrous ends.

These Mysteries were formerly taught, we are told, "on the highest hills and in the lowest valleys," which

God Father measuring the universe. Bible Moralisé, perhaps from Reims, France, mid-13th century.
Photo: Erich Lessing / Art Resource, NY.
Oesterreichische Nationalbibliothek, Vienna, Austria.

is merely a figure of speech for saying, first, that they have been taught in circumstances of the greatest seclusion and secrecy, and secondly, that they have been taught in both advanced and simple forms according to the understanding of their disciples. It is, of course, common knowledge that the great systems of the Mysteries (referred to in our lectures as "noble orders of architecture," i.e. of soul-building) existed in the East, in Chaldea, Assyria, Egypt, Greece, Italy, amongst the Hebrews, amongst Mahommedans and amongst Christians. All the great teachers of humanity, Socrates, Plato, Pythagoras, Moses, Aristotle, Virgil, the author of the Homeric poems, and the great Greek tragedians, along with St. John, St. Paul and innumerable other great names— were initiates of the Sacred Mysteries. The form of the teaching communicated varies considerably from age to age; it has been expressed under different veils; but since the ultimate truth the Mysteries aim at teaching is always one and the same, there has always been taught, and can only be taught, one and the same doctrine—for the moment let me merely say that behind all the official religious systems of the world, and behind all the great moral movements and developments in the history of humanity, have stood what St. Paul called the keepers or "stewards of the Mysteries." From that source Christianity itself came into the world. From them originated the great school of Kabalism, that marvelous system of secret, oral tradition of the Hebrews, a strong element of which has been introduced into our Masonic system. From them, too, also issued many fraternities and orders. Such for instance, as the great orders of Chivalry and of the Rosicrucians, and the school of spiritual alchemy. Lastly, from them too also issued, in the seventeenth century, modern speculative Freemasonry.

To trace the genesis of the movement, which came into activity some 250 years ago (our rituals and ceremonies having been compiled round the year 1700), is beyond the purpose of my present remarks. It may merely be stated that the movement itself incorporated the slender ritual and the elementary symbolism that, for centuries previously, had been employed in connection with the medieval Building Guilds, but it gave

to them a far fuller meaning and a far wider scope. It has always been the custom from Trade Guilds, and even for modern Friendly Societies, to spiritualize their trades, and to make the tools of their trade point to some simple moral. No trade, perhaps, lends itself more readily to such treatment than the builder's trade; but wherever a great industry has flourished, there you will find traces of that industry becoming allegorized, and of the allegory being employed for the simple moral instruction of those who were operative members of the industry. I am acquainted, for instance with an Egyptian ceremonial system, some 5,000 years old, which taught precisely the same things as Masonry does, but in terms of shipbuilding instead of in terms of architecture. But the terms of architecture were employed by those who originated modern Masonry because they were ready to hand; because they were in use among certain trade-guilds then in existence; and lastly, because they are extremely effective and significant from the symbolic point of view.

All that I wish to emphasize at this stage is that our present system is not one coming from remote antiquity: that there is no direct continuity between us and the Egyptians, or even the ancient Hebrews who built, in the reign of King Solomon, a certain Temple at Jerusalem. What is extremely ancient in Freemasonry is the spiritual doctrine concealed within the architectural phraseology; for this doctrine is an elementary form of the doctrine that has been taught in all ages, no matter in what garb.

HIDDEN IN PLAIN SIGHT

Freemasonry is "a system of morality veiled in allegory and illustrated by symbols."

It is the glory of God to conceal a thing; But the honor of kings is to search out a matter. —*Proverbs 25.2*

Langdon smiled. "Sorry, but the word occult, despite conjuring images of devil worship, actually means 'hidden' or 'obscured.' In times of religious oppression, knowledge that was counterdoctrinal had to be kept hidden or 'occult,' and because the church felt threatened by this, they redefined anything 'occult' as evil, and the prejudice survived." —*The Lost Symbol*

"As above, so below." These words, attributed to Hermes Trismegistus, lie at the heart of the Western esoteric tradition. In brief, they mean that the universe and all it contains is reflected in some manner not only on Earth, but also in man and his works. The chief quest of all ages has been man's attempt to understand the mystery of existence and to find his place in it.
—*C. Fred Kleinknecht, 33rd Degree, Sovereign Grand Commander, The Supreme Council*

After the collapse of the pagan cultural institutions, it was unlawful to teach classical learning or to advance scientific knowledge contrary to the prevailing scholasticism. To avoid persecution and at the same time perpetuate for the benefit of qualified disciples the more advanced formulas of the ancient wisdom, the sacred truths were presented symbolically. —*Manly P. Hall*

Speculative Masonry *by Jasper Ridley*

Jasper Ridley is a historian and biographer. His works include biographies of Mussolini, Tito, Henry VIII, Elizabeth I, Garibaldi, and Napoleon III and his wife, Eugenie. This excerpt comes from The Freemasons.

Between about 1550 and 1700, the Freemasons changed. They ceased to be an illegal trade union of working masons who accepted all the doctrines of the Catholic Church, and became an organization of intellectual gentlemen who favored religious toleration and friendship between men of different religions, and thought that a simple belief in God should replace controversial theological doctrines. In the language of the time, the "operative masons" were replaced by "admitted masons" or "gentlemen masons" as they were usually called in Scotland. In later times these admitted masons were called *speculative masons*, but this term was not used before 1757.[1]

No one really knows how this change came about. Masonic historians have written long and learned books giving their explanations, which have been refuted by other Masonic historians in equally long and learned books,

while the anti-Masonic writers, with their popular best-sellers, have put forward their own theories. Some of the explanations have been far-fetched and almost ridiculous. Others have been very convincing and are supported by a great deal of plausible evidence, but there is equally strong evidence which suggests that the explanation is wrong.

There is a long tradition of trade guilds accepting as members men who had no connection with the trade. The livery companies of the City of London—the oldest one was the Weavers, which was founded in 1155—originally consisted of members of the trade. But from the earliest times the liverymen's sons, if they had been born after their father joined the livery, could become liverymen by patrimony. In the Middle Ages a man usually followed his father's trade, but sometimes he did not; and this did not prevent him from joining the livery. Apart from this, the livery companies could admit as liverymen men who had no connection with the company, either by birth or occupation; and they often did so.

By the fourteenth century the great livery company, the Taylors and Linen

Armorers (who later changed their name to "the Merchant Taylors") were admitting as liverymen country gentlemen who sold them wool for export to the Netherlands. They even admitted King Edward III as a liveryman, after they had lent him money to pay for his wars which they knew he would never repay. For the gentlemen, it was an advantage to become more closely associated with the City of London, while for the livery company there was great social prestige in having gentlemen members in the very regimented society of fourteenth-century England with its class distinctions—gentlemen who, unlike their social inferiors, were allowed, if they owned land worth 20 pounds a year, to wear a gold ring, a silk shirt, and red or velvet garments.

In Scotland, it was very usual for influential gentlemen to be invited to join a trade guild. It became so common for the Scottish masons to invite the gentlemen of the St. Clair family at Rosslyn to join their guild, that the St. Clairs wrongly claimed that they had a hereditary right to exercise authority over the masons of Scotland. King James IV joined the Edinburgh Guild of Merchants in 1505; and sixty years later the Earl of Moray, the illegitimate half-brother of Mary Queen of Scots, when Regent for the infant King James VI, joined the Bakers' Company in Glasgow.[2]

By the sixteenth and seventeenth centuries, it was reading the Bible which made so many gentlemen wish to join the masonic lodges. The Catholic Church had rightly regarded the translation of the Bible into English, and the reading of the English Bible by the people, as the greatest threat to its authority. Sir Thomas More and other official persecutors had been zealous in burning copies of the English Bible and the Protestants who distributed them. If people read the Bible, they would regard the Bible, not the Church, as the authority which they must obey.

It was not good enough for the Church to tell the people that they must obey the Pope because it was stated in the Gospels that Christ had said to St. Peter: *"Tu es Petrus, et super hanc petram aedificabo ecclesiam mean"*[3]—a pun which was lost in the English translation "Thou are Peter, and upon this rock I will build my Church"; for the readers of the Bible could question why this passage meant that 1,500 years later, the Bishop of Rome was Supreme Head of the Church. They would point out that there was nothing in the Bible that stated that Peter was ever at Rome, just as they pointed out that Christmas should not be celebrated as a feast of the Church because there was nothing in the Bible that said that Our Lord was born on the twenty-fifth day of December. There were passages in the Bible which had revolutionary implications, as John Knox pointed out in his lengthy marginal notes in the English translation of the Bible which he and his colleagues published in Geneva in 1560. These passages showed that the prophets of God had deposed wicked kings, and, in Knox's words, that "Jehu killed two Kings at God's commandment."[4]

The Protestants read every ONE of the 860,000 words in the Bible to find texts which would denigrate the doctrines and authority of the Catholic Church. In the Second Book of Chronicles they read of how King Solomon decided to build a temple, how he asked Hiram, King of Tyre, to send him architects and masons to work on the temple, of how the work was completed; and they read about the length, width and height of the temple.[5] As everything in the Bible was the Word of God, these measurements were not inserted unnecessarily, or to satisfy the idle curiosity of the reader; they must have some profound theological implications.

Although the Presbyterians and the Protestant extremists rejected anything which was not in the Bible, the masons were prepared to add many stories, which were not in the Book of Chronicles, about the building of Solomon's temple. They told the story, not of Hiram, King of Tyre, but of another Hiram—Hiram Abiff, who knew the secret of the temple. Three villains kidnapped him and threatened him with death if he did not reveal it; and as he would not betray his trust, they murdered him. When Solomon found out about this, he wondered what was Hiram Abiff's secret, and if it had died with him. He sent three masons to find Hiram's body and the secret, and told them that if they could not discover the secret, the first thing that they saw when they found Hiram's body should henceforth be the secret of the temple. The masons eventually found Hiram's body, and when they opened his coffin, the first thing they found was his hand; and as they did not find the secret, the handshake and the other signs of recognition which the masons henceforth adopted became the new secret.[6]

As part of the ceremony in which a Freemason is raised to the third degree and becomes a master mason, he

KING NIMROD, THE FIRST AND MOST EXCELLENT MASTER?

Tower of Babel, 1563. Pieter Brueghel the Elder. *Kunsthistorisches Museum / Vienna, Austria.*

"The date of the construction of King Solomon's Temple has not always been the key date in the Freemasons' cosmology," wrote Daniel Beresniak in *Les symboles de Francs-maçons,* translated by Ian Monk). According to the Regius Manuscript (circa 1410), it was King Nimrod, builder of the Tower of Babel, "who gave the Masons their first 'charge,' their first rules of conduct and professional code." It wasn't until the early years of the eighteenth century that Nimrod was supplanted by Solomon.

participates in the reenactment of the story of the murder of Hiram Abiff. He swore an oath that, like Hiram, he would not reveal the Freemasons' secrets, and agreed that if he broke his oath, it would be right to put him to death by cutting out his heart, liver and other entrails. The horrific penalties which the candidate agreed should be inflicted on him if he broke his vow of secrecy bear a close resemblance to the punishment which traitors endured in the disemboweling part of the sentence of hanging, drawing and quartering.

The Masonic tradition told other stories about the origin and development of Freemasonry. In 1723, after the formation of the English Grande Lodge, they were published by the prominent Freemason, James Anderson, in his *Book of Constitutions;* but they were almost certainly circulating, and believed, before the end of the seventeenth century. God Himself was a mason; had He not built heaven and earth in six days? Adam was a mason. It was masons who built the Tower of Babel; and when God had ordained that the peoples should speak different languages, He had told the masons to communicate by secret signs with masons who spoke different languages. Noah was a mason, though he had built the ark of wood, not stone. Abraham was a mason. He invented geometry, and when he was in Egypt he met a Greek slave named Euclid. Abraham taught Euclid geometry, and Euclid wrote down what Abraham had told him, and through Euclid's writings the world learned geometry.

The story continued: masonry was introduced into Britain in Roman times by St. Alban; but after the death of the Four Crowned Martyrs it disappeared from Britain until it was reintroduced by King Athelstan in York in the tenth century. It was afterwards protected by other sovereigns. Queen Elizabeth I did not like the masons because, being a woman, she could not be admitted as one of them; but James I, Charles I, Charles II and William III were masons. Obviously masons were something very special, and God's favorites; just as God had created men to be above the animals, so He had created masons to be above other men.[7]

All this was absolute nonsense; but it was flattering to the masons, who believed what they wished to believe.

The learned men of the seventeenth century were greatly interested in Solomon's temple. Theologians, philosophers and other scholars wrote long books about it in Latin. The mathematician and scientist, Issac Newton, was particularly impressed by the temple. Many of his 470 books and writings are on theological subjects, and he wrote several about the temple. He considered that Solomon was the greatest philosopher of all time. He

SUFI ORIGINS   *by Robert Graves*

Most Masons will be surprised by this version of the origin of Freemasonry, by the author of **The White Goddess.**

The Sufis are an ancient spiritual freemasonry whose origins have never been traced or dated; nor do they themselves take much interest in such researches, being content to point out the occurrence of their own way of thought in different regions and periods....

Indeed, Freemasonry itself began as a Sufi society. It first reached England in the reign of King Aethelstan (924–939) and was introduced into Scotland disguised as a craft guild at the beginning of the fourteenth century, doubtless by the Knights Templars. Its reformation in early eighteenth-century London, by a group of Protestant sages who mistook its Saracen terms for Hebrew, has obscured many of its early traditions. Richard Burton...being both a Freemason and a Sufi, first pointed out the close relation between the two societies, but he was not sufficiently advanced in either to realize the Freemasons had begun as a Sufi group. Idries Shah Sayed now shows that it was a metaphor for the "reedification," or rebuilding of spiritual man from his ruined state; and that the three working instruments displayed on modern

Masonic lodges represent three postures of prayer. "Buizz" or "Boaz" and "Solomon, Son of David," who are honored by Freemasons as builders at King Solomon's temple at Jerusalem, were not Solomon's Israelite subjects or Phoenician allies as it is supposed, but Abdel-Malik's Sufi architects who built the Dome of the Rock on the ruins of Solomon's temple, and their successors. Their real names included Thuban abdel Faiz ("Izz"), and his "great grandson," Maaruf, the son (disciple) of David of Tay, whose Sufic code name was Solomon, because he was the "son of David." The architectural measurements chosen for this Temple, as for the Kaaba building at Mecca, were numerical equivalents of certain Arabic roots conveying holy messages, every part of the building being related to every other in definite proportion.

Omar Mosque dome (Dome of the Rock), Jerusalem, Israel. *Photo: S. Vannini © DeA Picture Library / Art Resource, NY.*

seems to have believed that his reading about the measurements of Solomon's temple had helped him to formulate his law of gravity and he was sure that from these measurements it was possible to foretell that Christ's Second Coming would take place in 1948, and the dates of other portentous events during the next four hundred years.[8]

Frontispiece to *The History of the Royal-Society of London* by Thomas Sprat, 1667. Designed by John Evelyn, engraved by Wenceslaus Hollar. Founded after the Restoration of Charles II in 1660, the Royal Society was guided by the scientific philosophies of Sir Francis Bacon. From left to right: William Brouncker, mathematician and first president of the society; bust of King Charles II; Sir Francis Bacon, who died in 1626.

And there was also the Mason Word. The people had heard about the Mason Word, and wondered what it was. There was no good reason why they should be interested to know the code word which the Scottish masons had invented to enable them to distinguish between master masons and entered apprentices; but after the people had read and heard about Solomon's temple and all the stories about the secret initiation ceremony and the oath taken by the Freemasons, the Mason Word acquired a romantic and sinister fascination. They had also heard about the Rosicrucians—the brethren of the "Rosy Cross," as they called them—and confused the Freemasons, the Rosicrucians, and witchcraft. A poem published in Edinburgh in 1638 referred to the Freemasons of Perth:

> For we be brethren of the Rosie
>   Cross;
> We have the Mason Word and
>   second sight;
> Things for to come we can foretell
>   aright.[9]

The Presbyterian minister of a parish in Kirkcudbrightshire was worried in 1695 about the connection between Freemasonry and witchcraft. He had been informed that a local mason had met with the Devil, and had donated his first child to him in return for being told the Mason Word: but after investigating the matter, the minister was convinced that the allegation was untrue, that the mason had never encountered the Devil, and did not know the Mason Word.[10]

Sir Robert Moray was one of the few men who had links with both the Rosicrucians and the Freemasons. He was a good Presbyterian, but, like other Scottish gentlemen of an adventurous disposition, he went to France in the 1630s and volunteered for the army of the Catholic King Louis XIII. Louis' Prime Minister, Cardinal Richelieu, sent him to fight with the French army on the Protestant side in the Thirty Years War, because Richelieu thought that it was in the national interest of France to oppose the Hapsburg Holy Roman Empire and the King of Spain. After distinguished service in the French army, Moray returned to Scotland and fought for the Scottish Covenanters when they revolted against the attempts of Charles I and Archbishop Laud to force them adopt a less Protestant form of Church service than that laid down in John Knox's service book. The Scots were victori-

ous, and invaded England. While their army was stationed at Newcastle, Moray, who was Quarter-Master-General of the army, was initiated on 20 March 1641 into an Edinburgh masonic lodge, some of whose members were at Newcastle with the army. It was the first recorded case of admission to a military lodge which afterwards became a common practice in the army.[11]

The Scots won their war against Charles I, and Charles's defeat precipitated the revolution of 1640 and the outbreak of the Civil War in England. The Scots at first remained neutral in the English Civil War, and then came in on the side of Parliament against the King on condition that Parliament made England a Presbyterian state; but Robert Moray, like the Marquess of Montrose, was one of the minority of Presbyterians who, having fought against Charles I in the war of 1640, fought on Charles's side in the English Civil War. After Charles's defeat and capture, Moray escaped to France, but returned to England at the Restoration of Charles II, and was one of the founders of the Royal Society. Moray was a friend and patron of Thomas Vaughan, the Welch Rosicrucian, who published the first English translation of Fama Fraternitatis, which was supposed to have been written by Christian Rosenkrantz.[12]

The English antiquarian, Elias Ashmole, whose collection founded the Ashmolean Museum in Oxford, was a London solicitor. He fought for Charles I in the Civil War, and at the end of the war in 1646 he was taken prisoner by the Roundheads in Lancashire. While he was a prisoner he was initiated as a Freemason at Warrington on 16 October 1646. His father-in-law, Colonel Henry Mainwaring, who was an officer in the Roundhead army and a landowner in Cheshire, was initiated into the lodge at the same time. Ashmole continued all his life to be interested in Freemasonry, and recorded in his diary that he attended a meeting of a Freemason's lodge in the halls of the Masons' Company of London in 1682.[13]

Masonic lodges, with accepted masons as members, were spreading all over England. Robert Plot, the Keeper of the Ashmolean Museum and professor of chemistry at Oxford University, who was not a Freemason, wrote about Freemasonry in his native county in his *Natural History of Stafford-shire* in 1686. He noted that it was spreading all over England, but faster in the moorlands of Stafford-shire than elsewhere:

for here I found persons of the most eminent quality, that did not disdain to be of their *Fellowship*. Nor indeed need they, were of that *Antiquity* and *honor*, that is pretended in a large parchment volume they have amongst them, containing the *History* and *Rules* of the craft of *masonry*.[14]

In London, some eminent intellectuals, and several members of the Royal Society, were Freemasons; but many were not. Ashmole, Sir Robert Moray, and perhaps Inigo Jones, were Freemasons, but Issac Newton was not. There has been a great dispute as to whether Sir Christopher Wren was a Freemason, and the evidence is contradictory; but a recently discovered document seems to confirm that he was initiated as a Freemason in 1691, but never played an active part in the affairs of the craft.[15]

In Scotland, too, more gentlemen masons were joining. John Boswell, the laird of Auchinleck, who was initiated as a member of an Edinburgh lodge on 8 June 1600, may have been admitted merely because the masons thought it useful to have a gentlemen as a member of their lodge; but in a lodge in Aberdeen in 1670, of the 49 master masons only 10 were operative masons; 4 were noble-men, 3 were gentlemen, 8 were lawyers and professional men, 9 were merchants, and 15 were tradesmen.[16]

Another theory has been put forward to explain the growth of Freemasonry in Scotland. This claims that the Free-masons were the Knights Templars, the military order which had been estab-lished to defend the Christian kingdom in Palestine. In 1094 the Pope launched the First Crusade, calling on Christian Europe to liberate Jerusalem, the city where Christ had lived and died, from the Muslim infidels. In July 1099 the Crusaders captured Jerusalem, and massacred most of the Muslim inhabit-ants of the city. They then established a Christian kingdom in Jerusalem and the surrounding country which they caller Outremer.

It was of course necessary to defend the kingdom of Outremer against the attempts of the Muslims to recapture it, and in 1118 the Pope authorized the for-mation of a body of military knights who were called the Knights Templars. For 160 years Knights Templars defended Outremer against the Muslims, but with only partial success. In 1187 the Muslims, under their leader Saladin, overran Outremer and captured Jerusalem; and

all the attempts of the Crusaders to re-capture it were unsuccessful until the Holy Roman Emperor, Frederick II, went on the Sixth Crusade in 1228, at a time when he was engaged in a bitter power struggle against the Pope, who had excommunicated him and was of-fering financial help to the Muslims to enable them to defeat the Emperor's cru-sade. But Frederick, whose tolerant at-titude on religious questions made him as willing to enter into friendly nego-tiations with the Muslims as he was with the Jews, made a treaty with the Sultan which gave him the right to occupy Damascus, Nazareth and Jerusalem for ten years; and without fighting a battle he became the only Christian leader to enter Jerusalem since Saladin captured it. While Pope Gregory IX committed the great sin of invading the territory of a ruler who was absent on a cru-sade, and ravaged Frederick's provinces in Northern Italy, Frederick crowned himself King of Jerusalem, as no bishop or priest was willing to crown him in view of the Pope's censures.

At the expiry of the ten-year treaty, the Muslims reentered Jerusalem in 1239, and no Christian crusader ever en-tered it again. The next crusade was led by a far more pious and obedient son of the Church than Frederick II—by St. Louis, King of France, who told his favorite, Jean, Sieur de Joinville, that the only way in which a good Christian should argue with a Jew was by driving his sword up to the hilt into the Jew's entrails. St. Louis' two crusades failed. The last Crusade was abandoned in 1276. After this, there was nothing left for the Knights Templars to do.

During their stay in Outremer, the Templars had been in contact with Muslims and Jews, and became interested in their legends. They learned the stories about the building of Solomon's temple in Jerusalem. Some of them, like the members of other medieval monastic orders, became corrupted. The rumor spread that they engaged in unnatural vices, including homosexuality, and that they indulged in satanic anti-Christian practices; it was said that when new recruits joined the Templars, they spat on the crucifix during their initiation ceremonies, and denied Christ.

In 1305 King Philip IV of France (Philippe le Bel) decided to suppress the Templars and seize all their valuable property. Two Templars confessed to the authorities that they had indulged in immoral and satanic practices. The Pope was skeptical; for two years he refused to believe the King's allegations against the Templars. But as more and more of the arrested Knights Templars confessed their crimes, he agreed to order a thorough investigation of the Order. The Inquisitors interrogated more than 500 Templars and other witnesses in France; but they also pursued their inquiries in other countries, including England, where they examined 68 witnesses in London, Lincoln and York. In Scotland, 2 Templars and 41 other witnesses were questioned by the Bishop of St. Andrews.

The Templars were found guilty of most of the crimes of which they were accused. The aged Grand Master, Jacques de Molay, and three of his highest officers eventually confessed, and after being held in prison for many months they were brought before the cardinals in the cathedral of Notre Dame in Paris on 11 March 1314, and sentenced to life imprisonment. Two of them accepted the judgment of the court, but Molay and the Provincial Grand Master of Normandy retracted their confessions, proclaimed that they were innocent of all the crimes with which they were charged, and that they deserved to die for having falsely accused their Order. The cardinals adjourned the proceedings till next day, saying that they would then deal with the two obstinate Templars; but news of what had happened was brought to King Philippe le Bel in his nearby palace of the Louvre. He ordered that Molay and the Provincial Grand Master of Normandy should immediately be burned alive as relapsed heretics on a little island in the River Seine between the royal gardens and the church of the Hermit Brothers of St. Augustine; and the sentence was carried out the same evening.[17]

Although most of the Knights Templars were executed, sentenced to long terms of imprisonment, or pardoned after confessing their crimes, there is no doubt that some of them disappeared and escaped. What happened to them? All that is definitively known is that the King of Portugal, unlike the other European sovereigns, found the Templars not guilty of the charges against them. He granted political asylum to those of them who reached Portugal, and allowed them to reconstitute themselves under another name.

But in later centuries other rumors spread about the Knights Templars. It was said that old Jacques de Molay, though suffering from the effects of torture, was in full possession of his senses in the final days before he was burned.

He succeeded in summoning a secret meeting of his higher officers in his prison cell and appointed four deputies who were to continue governing the Order in the South, the North, the East, and the West. The South was to be governed from Paris, the North from Stockholm, the East from Naples, and the West from Edinburgh.[18] Some of the Templars escaped to Scotland, where Robert Bruce was conducting his war of independence against King Edward II of England, and had been excommunicated by the Pope for having killed his rival claimant to the throne, Comyn, in a church. Bruce secretly granted asylum to the Knights Templars.

On 24 June 1314—three months after Molay and his companion were burned—Bruce defeated Edward II at the Battle of Bannockburn. Our knowledge of precisely what happened at Bannockburn is a little hazy, because the earliest surviving account was written by a Scottish chronicler nearly sixty years later; but according to his story, at the decisive moment in the battle, the Scottish "ghillies"—the servants who carried out routine duties in the Scottish camp—walked to the top of the hill overlooking the battlefield to see what was going on. The English saw them, and, wrongly believing that a new Scottish army was about to join the battle, ran away. According to another theory, this new army was not the camp ghillies, but the Knights Templars to whom Bruce had granted asylum; they now showed their gratitude to Bruce by fighting for him at Bannockburn.

After the battle the Knights Templars took refuge in one of the islands off the west coast of Scotland. They stayed there for eighty years, but at the end of the fourteenth century moved to the east coast and settled in Aberdeen, where they called themselves the Freemasons. By the sixteenth century they had moved again, going south to Edinburgh.[19]

THE LEGEND OF HIRAM ABIFF

He was a widow's son of the tribe of Naphtali.—I Kings 7: 13-14

Gerard de Nerval
(1808–1855)
Photo:
Adoc-photos/
Art Resource, NY.

In 1851, the French poet Gerard de Nerval, having just returned from what was then an exotic Middle East, published (a memoir, which has been translated as Journey to the Orient). In this opus, Nerval included…travelogue, commentaries on manners and mores, legends he had encountered, folk tales and stories he had heard. Among the latter, there is the fullest, most detailed, and most evocative version of the Hiram story ever to appear in print, either before or after. Nerval not only recited the basic narrative…[but] also divulged—for the first time, to our knowledge—a skein of eerie mystical traditions associated in Freemasonry with Hiram's background and pedigree…[Nerval's] weird, haunting, and evocative retelling is the most complete and detailed version we have, or are likely ever to have.

—*Michael Baigent and Richard Leigh,*
The Temple and the Lodge

The Lost Word
by Gerard de Nerval

(Hiram is referred to as Adoniram in this telling; Daoud is David and Saba is Sheba. NB: The queen of Sheba's visit to Solomon is recounted in the First Book of Kings.)

While Soliman welcomed Balkis at his country residence, a man, crossing the heights of Moriah, looked pensively at the twilight dwindling in the clouds and at the blazing tapers which pierced the shadows around Millo like a multitude of stars. He bid his beloved a silent farewell and took a last look at the rocks of Solyme and the banks of Kedron. The weather was cloudy, and before the pallid sun fully set, it had time to see the night advancing upon the earth. At the noise of the hammers on the bronze bells, sounding the call to muster, Adoniram struggled

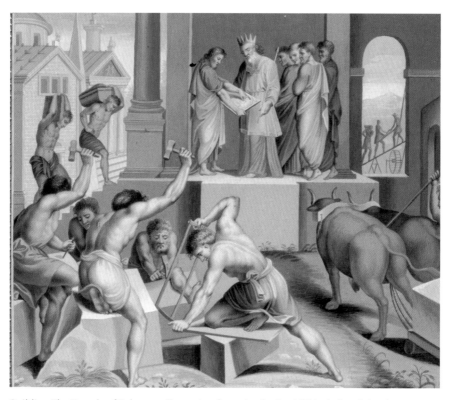

Building The Temple of Solomon, illustration from the Raphael Bible, Italian School, 18th century. *Private Collection. Photo © Bonhams, London, UK / The Bridgeman Art Library.*

KING SOLOMON'S TEMPLE AND THE LEGEND OF HIRAM ABIFF

Construction of the Temple of Solomon (also known as "The First Temple") was completed in 960 B.C. It was located on the east side of Jerusalem on Mount Moriah. The building of the temple is described in detail in the Bible. Its principal function was to house the Ark of the Covenant, which contained the sacred tablets given to Moses by God. Hiram, King of Tyre, supplied Solomon with materials and many skilled workers for the project, including the Master Builder, Hiram Abiff.

According to the legend, Hiram determined whether each worker was an Apprentice, Fellow, or Master through a system of secret words, enabling him to pay them the appropriate salary. The Apprentice word was "Boaz," the Fellow word was "Jachin," and the Master word was "Jehovah." ("Boaz" and "Jachin" are commemorated in all Masonic lodges as two pillars symbolizing duality.)

The legend continues that one day three evil workers attacked Hiram and demanded to know the Master word. When he refused, they murdered him, buried his body in the countryside, and fled. It is said that during the course of his struggle with his assailants Hiram cried out, "Is there no help for the widow's son?" Hiram's refusal to divulge the secret word—at the cost of his life—has been revered by Freemasons as an example of courage and steadfastness in the face of danger.

Baigent and Leigh commend a very intriguing version of the Hiram legend, in which his wife was the Queen of Sheba, and King Solomon coveted her.

Is Nerval's version credible? Perfectly, as allegory. (How can you doubt the veracity of a man who was fond of walking his pet lobster, Thibault, through the gardens at the Palais Royal at the end of a long blue ribbon?)

Construction of the Temple of Jerusalem under the Order of Solomon, Jean Fouquet (c.1415/20–1481). *Bibliothèque Nationale, Paris, France. Giraudon / Art Resource, NY.*

free of his thoughts and hastened on his way. Soon he passed through the crowd of assembled workmen to preside over the distribution of salaries. He entered the temple through the west door and emerged at the partly open east door to place himself at the foot of the column of Jachin.

Lighted tapers below the peristyle crackled under drops of tepid rain to which the panting workmen merrily offered their sweating limbs. The crowd was large, and Adoniram had at his disposal, besides the book-keepers, stewards in charge of the different categories. To divide the workmen into the three hierarchical grades a watchword was used, replacing in these circumstances the hand signals which would have taken up too much time. Then the salaries were distributed on the declaration of the password.

The apprentices' watchword was Jachin, the journeymen's Boaz, and the masters' Jehovah. Arranged in their appropriate groups and lined up one behind the other, the workmen presented themselves to the stewards at the counting-house. Before each one received his wages, Adoniram touched his hand, and the workman whispered a word in his ear. The password had been changed for this final day. The apprentices said Tubal-Cain, the journeymen Shibboleth, and the masters Giblim.

Gradually the crowd thinned out, the precincts grew deserted, but when the last petitioner had withdrawn, it was clear that not all of the men had attended the ceremony, for there was still some money in one of the coffers.

"Tomorrow," Adoniram said to his stewards, "summon the men together again to discover whether they are ill or have been visited by death."

As soon as Adoniram's officers had left, Adoniram himself, zealous and vigilant to the last day, took hold of a lamp, as usual, to inspect the empty workshops and the various locales of the temple, to make sure that his orders had been executed and that the fires had been extinguished. His footsteps echoed sadly along the flagstones. Looking once more at his monuments, he stopped, for a long time, in front of a group of winged cherubim, the last work of the young Benoni.

"Sweet child," he sighed.

Once this pilgrimage was over, Adoniram found himself in the temple's huge hall. The dense shadows around his lamp unrolled into red volutes, revealing the high moldings on the vaults, and also the walls of the hall, the exits of which were three doors facing north, west, and east. The north door was reserved for the people, the west for the king and his warriors, the east for the Levites, and outside this latter door stood the bronze columns of Jachin and Boaz.

Before leaving by the west door, which was the nearest to him, Adoniram glanced at the dark recesses of the hall, and, deeply moved as he remained from looking at the innumerable statues, his imagination evoked the shade of Tubal-Cain in the shadows. Concentrating his gaze, he tried to penetrate the darkness; the phantom grew taller but glided away; it reached the very depths of the temple and vanished close to the walls, like the shadow of a man spotlighted by a torch which slowly withdraws. A woeful cry seemed to resound among the vaults. Then Adoniram turned round and prepared to depart.

Suddenly, a human form detached itself from the pilaster and said to him in a ferocious voice:

"If you wish to leave, tell me the password of the masters."

Adoniram carried no weapons upon him. Respected by everyone, accustomed to command by only a sign, he did not even dream of defending his sacred person.

"Wretch!" he exclaimed, recognizing the journeyman, the Hebrew Methuselah, "Step back at once! You will be welcomed among the masters on the day that crime and treachery are honored! Flee with your accomplices before the justice of Soliman falls upon your heads."

At these words, Methuselah lifted up his hammer in his muscular arms and brought it down with a crash upon Adoniram's skull. Stunned but still conscious, the artist staggered towards the north door, but the Syrian Phanor was waiting for him there.

"If you wish to leave, tell me the password of the masters."

"You have not worked for seven years," Adoniram managed to reply.

"The password!"

"Never!"

Phanor the mason thrust his chisel into Adoniram's entrails, but he was unable to aim a second blow, for aroused by the pain, the architect of the temple flew like an arrow towards the east door in order to escape from his assassins. There, the Phoenician Amrou, journeyman among the carpenters, was waiting for him, and he, too, cried out in his turn:

Freemason's rug from a lodge. Symbols include a masonic temple, trowel and hammer, columns of King Solomon's temple, a pair of compasses, T-square and sun and moon. 19th century. *Photo Credit: Erich Lessing / Art Resource, NY. Oesterreichisches Freimaurermuseum (Freemasons' Museum), Rosenau, Austria.*

"If you wish to leave, tell me the password of the masters!"

"This is not the way that I learned it myself," Adoniram gasped. "Request it from the one who sends you here."

As he strove to open the door, Amrou plunged the point of his compass into Adoniram's heart.

At that moment the storm erupted, heralded by a mighty stroke of thunder.

Stretched out upon the temple floor, Adoniram's body covered three flagstones. The three murderers reassembled at his feet and linked their hands together.

"This man was great," Phanor murmured.

"He won't take up more space in the tomb than you," Amrou said.

"May his blood fall upon Soliman ben Daoud!" Phanor exclaimed.

"Let us lament for ourselves," Methuselah added, "for we are masters of the king's secret. We must destroy all proof of the murder. The rain is pouring down and the night is as black as pitch. Come, let us quickly carry the corpse far away from the city and commit it to the earth."

Then they wrapped the corpse in a long apron of white leather, and, heaving it up in their arms, descended in silence to the banks of the Kedron, directing their steps towards a solitary spot beyond the route to Bethany. As they drew near to it, troubled as they were and shivering in their hearts, they suddenly found themselves confronted by an escort of horsemen. They halted in apprehension. And then the queen of Saba passed by the terror-stricken assassins who were hauling away the remains of her husband Adoniram.

When one of the escorts rode directly up to them, they were too dumbfounded to move, but he merely glanced at them, turned his horse aside and rejoined the procession which rapidly disappeared in the darkness. Then they went further away and dug a hole in the earth to conceal the corpse of the artist. When their work was done, Methuselah uprooted the trunk of a young acacia tree and replanted it in the newly turned-up soil under which their victim reposed.

During this time, as lightning continued to rend the sky, Balkis was fleeing across the valleys, and Soliman was sleeping. His wound was a cruel one, too, for he had to awake.

When the sun had turned completely round the earth, the lethargic effect of the philtre which he had drunk passed away. Tormented by nightmares, the king struggled against a host of visions, and he returned to the domain of the living with a violent shock.

He rises to his feet in astonishment; his bewildered eyes appear to search for their master's reason...and at length he remembers. The empty goblet stands before him and he recalls the queen's words: "I obey, I yield, I am yours!"...but unable to see her any longer he grows disturbed. A beam of sunlight which hovers

ironically upon his forehead makes him shudder....He divines everything, hurls the goblet to the floor and utters a cry of fury. He makes inquiries in vain. Nobody saw her leave the room. Her retinue, however, has disappeared from the plain, and nothing but the traces of her tents is left behind.

"So!" Soliman cried, casting a look of rage at Zadok, "so that is the kind of help which your god offers to his servants! Is that what he promised me? He delivers me up like a toy to the spirits of hell, and you, you imbecile of a minister who reign in his name owing to my impotence, you abandoned me, without foreseeing anything, without preventing anything! Who will give me winged legions to overtake this perfidious queen? Genii of the earth and fire, rebellious angels, spirits of the air, will you obey me?"

"Blasphemy!" Zadok rebuked him, raising his voice. "Jehovah alone is great, and he is a jealous God."

Just as Soliman was about to retort, the prophet Ahijah the Shilonite entered the room. Ascetic and awesome, he resembled a pure, disincarnate spirit; his features were somber and stern, his gaze acutely penetrating, and his eyes blazed with divine fire. Turning toward Soliman, he addressed him thus:

"'And the Lord said unto him, Therefore whosoever slayeth Cain, vengeance shall be taken on him sevenfold. And the Lord set a mark upon Cain, lest any finding him should kill him.' And Lamech, offspring of Cain, cried out to his wives: 'I have slain a man to my wounding, and a young man to my hurt. If Cain shall be avenged sevenfold, truly Lamech seventy and sevenfold.' Listen now, O king, to the words which the Lord commands me to declare unto thee: 'As for whosoever has shed the blood of Cain and of Lamech, vengeance shall be taken on him seven hundred and sevenfold!'" Soliman bowed his head; he remembered Adoniram and realized that his orders had been carried out. Overcome by remorse, he cried out:

"Wretches! What have they done? I did not tell them to kill him!"

Alone, abandoned by his God, at the mercy of the genii, reproved by Zadok, scorned by Ahijah, deceived by the queen of the Sabeans, driven ultimately to despair, Soliman glanced at his helpless hands. But at the sight of the talisman, he was aroused by a glimmer of hope, for the ring which he had received from Balkis still glittered on his finger, provoking him. He turned its stone towards the sun, and all the birds of the air flocked around him at once, except Hud-Hud, the magic hoopoe. He summoned her three times, thereby forcing her to comply, and then he commanded the bird to lead him to the queen. The hoopoe obediently took to wing, and Soliman, whose hands were stretched forth towards her, felt himself swept up from the floor and carried off through the air at an incredible speed. Gripped by terror, he turned his hand aside, and found himself safely back on the ground. The hoopoe, however, crossed the valley and alighted upon the summit of a hillock to settle on the frail branch of an acacia tree which was planted there. And none of Soliman's invocations would ever make her move again.

Seized by vertigo, the king dreamed of mustering innumerable armies to

> "If we recover our master from this pit," a third replied, "the first word which any one of us pronounces will serve as the password."

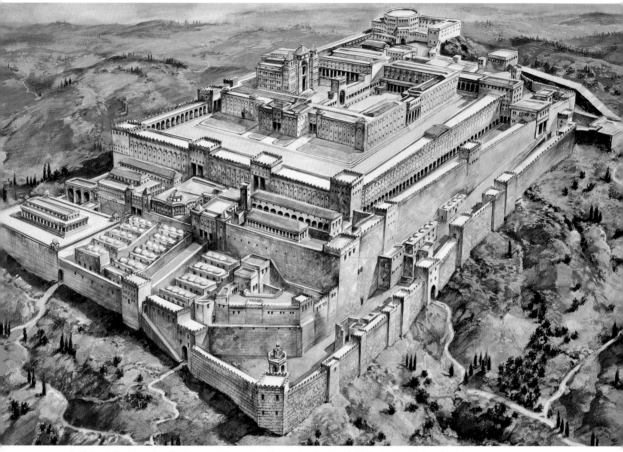

Building The Temple of Solomon, illustration from the Raphael Bible, Italian School, 18th century. Private Collection. *Photo © Bonhams, London, UK / The Bridgeman Art Library.*

devastate the kingdom of Saba, reduce it to ashes, and finally extinguish the flames with the blood of its inhabitants. He often locked himself up alone, cursed his fate and conjured up legions of spirits. An afrite, a genie of hell, was compelled to serve him and attend upon him in his solitude. In order to forget the queen and divert his fatal passion, Soliman had foreign women brought to him from every corner of the world. He married them in accordance with heathen rites, and they, in turn, initiated him in the idolatrous cult of images. Soon, to please the genii, he peopled the high places and raised, not far from Mount Tabor, a temple to Molech. The prophecy which Tubal-Cain had uttered in the kingdom of fire to his son Adoniram was thus confirmed: "You are destined to revenge us, and this temple you are raising to Adonai will cause the downfall of his faithful servant, Soliman."

But, as the Talmud informs us, the king of the Hebrews did not meet his doom so quickly. When the news of Adoniram's murder had spread far and wide, the people rose up and demanded justice. The king commanded nine of the masters to find Adoniram's grave in order to prove that he had in fact been assassinated.

Seventeen days passed. The search and investigations in the temple's environs led to nothing, neither did the examination of the surrounding countryside. Then, one of the masters, exhausted by the heat, attempted to seize hold of the branch of an acacia-tree so that he would be able to clamber up the mountain more easily. A brilliant bird of an unknown species, perched upon a branch of this tree, immediately flew away, and the master was astonished to discover that the whole trunk yielded now to his hand and no longer clung to the soil. The soil itself, he noticed, had been recently turned up, and he called to his companions to join him. Digging away with their hands and nails, the nine

masters soon perceived the shape of a grave.

"The criminals," one of them said, "are perhaps traitors who wanted to wrest the password of the masters from Adoniram. For fear that they succeeded, would it not be prudent to change it?"

"What word, then, should we adopt?" another asked.

"If we recover our master from this pit," a third replied, "the first word which any one of us pronounces will serve as the password. It will thereby perpetuate the memory of this crime and reinforce the vow we shall make to inflict vengeance for it, we and our children, upon the heads of the murderers and their remotest posterity."

Joining their hands together over the grave, the nine masters swore the vow, and dug up the soil with renewed vigor. Once the corpse had been identified, one of the masters touched it tenderly with his fingers, and the skin stuck to his hand. The same happened when the next one touched it. The third took hold of the wrist in the manner used by the masters to greet each other, and as even more skin broke loose this time, he cried out:

"Makbenash!" (The skin leaves the bones!)

All of them agreed that henceforth this would be the password of the masters and the rallying cry of Adoniram's avengers. Moreover, through the justice of God, this word also served for many centuries to rouse the people against the progeny of kings.

Phanor, Amrou, and Methuselah had taken flight. Recognized as false brothers, however, they were slain by workmen in the States of Maaca, king of the country of Gath, where they were hiding under the names of Sterkin, Oterfut, and Hoben.

For a long time afterwards, Adoniram's descendants were regarded as sacred by the workmen's guilds who would swear by The Sons of the Widow, thereby denoting the offspring of Adoniram and the queen of Saba.

Following the decree of Soliman ben Daoud, the illustrious artist was buried beneath the very altar of the temple which he had raised. Adonai therefore abandoned the ark of the Hebrews and reduced the successors of Daoud to bondage.

As Above, So Below   by Manly Palmer Hall

Dan Brown begins The Lost Symbol *with a quotation from* The Secret Teachings of All Ages *by Manly Palmer Hall: "To live in the world without becoming aware of the meaning of the world is like wandering about in a great library without touching the books." And he comes back to Hall at the very end of the book, when Langdon and Katherine are gazing up at* The Apotheosis of Washington, *"If the infinite had not desired man to be wise, he would not have bestowed upon him the faculty of knowing."*

Originally published in 1928 as An Encyclopedic Outline of Masonic, Hermetic, Qabbalistic and Rosicrucian Symbolical Philosophy, The Secret Teachings *remains "a classic in the world's literature; it will guide historians, philosophers, and lay seekers of esoteric wisdom for centuries," according to Edgar Mitchell.*

In 1934 Hall founded the Philosophical Research Foundation in Los Angeles, dedicated to "the ensoulment of all arts, sciences, and crafts, and devoted to the one basic purpose of advancing the brotherhood of all that lives, to meet all lovers of wisdom on a common ground." The PRS carries on, and their website (www.prs.org) is well worth a visit.

The story of CHiram may well represent the incorporation of the divine secrets of architecture into the actual parts and dimensions of earthly buildings. The three degrees of the Craft bury the Grand Master (the Great Arcanum) in the actual structure they erect, after first having *killed* him with the builder's tools, by reducing the dimensionless Spirit of Cosmic Beauty to the limitations of concrete form. These abstract ideals of architecture can be resurrected, however, by the Master Mason who, by meditating upon the structure, releases therefrom the divine principles of architectonic philosophy incorporated or buried within it. Thus the physical building is actually the tomb or embodiment of the Creative Ideal of which its material dimensions are but the shadow.

Moreover, the Hiramic legend may be considered to embody the vicissitudes of philosophy itself. As institutions for the dissemination of ethical culture, the pagan Mysteries were the architects of civilization. Their power and dignity were personified in CHiram Abiff—the Master Builder—but they eventually fell a victim to the onslaughts of that recurrent trio of state, church and mob. They were desecrated by the state, jealous of their wealth and power; by the early church, fearful of their wisdom; and by the rabble or soldiery incited by both state and church. As CHiram when *raised* from his grave whispers the Master Mason's Word which was lost through his untimely death, so according to the tenets of philosophy the re-establishment or resurrection of the ancient Mysteries will result in the rediscovery of that secret teaching without which civilization must continue in a state of spiritual confusion and uncertainty.

When the mob governs, man is ruled by ignorance; when the church governs, he is ruled by superstition; and when the state governs, he is ruled by fear. Before men can live together in harmony and understanding, ignorance must be transmuted into wisdom, superstition into an illumined faith, and fear into love. Despite statements to the contrary,

> When the mob governs, man is ruled by ignorance; when the church governs, he is ruled by superstition; and when the state governs, he is ruled by fear.

Masonry is a religion seeking to unite God and man by elevating its initiates to that level of consciousness whereon they can behold with clarified vision the workings of the Great Architect of the Universe. From age to age the vision of a perfect civilization is preserved as the ideal for mankind. In the midst of that civilization shall stand a mighty university wherein both the sacred and secular sciences concerning the mysteries of life will be freely taught to all who will assume the philosophic life. Here creed and dogma will have no place; the superficial will be removed and only the essential be preserved. The world will be ruled by its most illumined minds, and each will occupy the position for which he is most admirably fitted.

The great university will be divided into grades, admission to which will be through preliminary tests or initiations. Here mankind will be instructed in the most sacred, the most secret, and the most enduring of all Mysteries—

Symbolism. Here the initiate will be taught that every visible object, every abstract thought, every emotional reaction is but the symbol of an eternal principle. Here mankind will learn that CHiram (Truth) lies buried in every atom of Kosmos; that every form is a symbol and every symbol the tomb of an eternal verity. Through education—spiritual, mental, moral, and physical—man will learn to release living truths from their lifeless coverings. The perfect government of the earth must be patterned eventually after that divine government by which the universe is ordered. In that day when perfect order is reestablished, with peace universal and good triumphant, men will no longer seek for happiness, for they shall find it welling up within themselves. Dead hopes, dead aspirations, dead virtues shall rise from their graves, and the Spirit of Beauty and Goodness repeatedly slain by ignorant men shall again be the Master of Work. Then shall sages sit upon the seats of the mighty and the gods walk with men.

Symbolic Masonry   *by John J. Robinson*

John J. Robininson was the author of Born in Blood: The Lost Secrets of Freemasonry *and* Dungeon, Fire and Sword: The Knights Templar in the Crusades, *and* A Pilgrim's Path.

In searching for answers in the allegory known as the legend of Hiram Abiff, it was necessary to bear in mind that in Secret Masonry the Master Mason was a master of men, not a master of an art or craft. The bulk of the Masonic order had been made up of Fellows, the full members, and of Entrants, those whose discretion and trustworthiness were not yet acceptable enough to merit their invitation to full membership. Most of those Entrants would have known only those brother Masons who were in their own cell, or lodge. The Masters were the masters of

> As we search British history to find an unfinished temple as a basis for an exclusively British secret society, we find just one answer, in the religious order that often called itself by that simple name alone: the Temple.

territory or of lodges, which required that they maintain communication with one another. This communication, and even the occasional secret general assembly, would have been absolutely necessary for the important matter of standardization—for arriving at common agreements as to hand and arm signals, passwords, and catechisms by means of which a brother Mason could seek help and by which members could identify one another with some sense of security. When it is even suspected in a secret society that security has been breached, those secret signs must be changed, with meetings held to make the change and then to spread the word. Also, in order to direct a brother on the run to the next lodge, it was obviously necessary that someone know the locations of those other lodges, at least on a regional basis. Thus, the Masters were at the same time the most important and the most dangerous members of the fraternity. Brothers whose acquaintances were limited to their own individual cells could betray no more than the membership of that single cell, whether in their cups or on the rack; but a Master could jeopardize the very existence of the society by revealing the names of other Masters, all of whom possessed much broader information, including the names and locations of still other Masters. That would be the reason why only the Master had need for a Grand Hailing Sign of Distress and a special call for help when in the dark, or just out of sight of assistance: "Oh, Lord my God, is there no help for a Son of the Widow?"

Every Master was the "widow's son." He was the continuation of the Master-line that had apparently been broken with the death of the first Grand Master, Hiram Abiff. In the initiation drama he had been assigned the role of Hiram Abiff, whose mantle, thus assumed, became the central feature of the candidate's role in the secret society. In that same role he would emulate Abiff, who died rather than give up the secrets of the Master Mason. In that role he would

thwart the effects of the attack by three assassins who had wanted those secrets badly enough to kill, not caring that the murder of Hiram Abiff meant an end to the building of the unfinished temple.

That continuation of the function of the Grand Master and temple architect, a kind of immortalization of a dream kept alive by those to come after him, was symbolized by the branch of acacia, a symbol of immortality much older than Christianity. To ancient peoples, the weather and the reactions of crops were the determinates of life and death, of good living or near starvation during the year ahead. The changes in seasons, too much or too little rain, and crop-killing frosts were much more understandable and more easily addressed in religious worship than were total mysteries such as molds, fungi, and animal diseases, which were usually ascribed to witchcraft or the evil eye. With no fresh food to look forward to and no means to preserve the food they had, the most dreaded season was winter, when the days grew shorter as the Power of Darkness each day gained ground over the Power of Light. As though to maximize their misery, every bush, tree, and plant died. All, that is, except the evergreen. It stayed bright and green and so had to be occupied by a spirit stronger than the Power of Darkness, preserving life until the sun could manage its inevitable, but temporary, victory. That strong spirit helped to bridge the gap from autumn to spring, preserving the thread of life. In some areas, an evergreen tree was cut down in order to bring the good spirit into the house, where the branches were draped with gifts, a tradition of the old natural religion which we still preserve at Christmastime. Thus the evergreen became a symbol of immortality, and one of those evergreens was the acacia.

The acacia would have been selected as the symbol of Hiram Abiff's "immortality" for very specific reasons. It was of acacia wood that God ordered that the Ark of the Covenant be made, the ark that was to be housed in the Sanctum Sanctorum of Solomon's temple, where the Grand Master made his plans for the next day's work. The acacia was also the

Five hundred years after the Templar suppression, popes were still condemning Freemasonry for welcoming members of all religious faiths and for failing to acknowledge Roman Catholicism as the one true church.

host of a special breed of mistletoe with a flame-red flower. Not only was that mistletoe—which not only stayed green, but actually bore its fruit in the winter—a strong symbol of immortality in itself, but many believe that the acacia, covered with a blanket of fiery mistletoe blossoms, was the "burning bush" of the Old Testament. In addition the Egyptian acacia bears a red and white flower, a reminder of the Templar colors based upon a white mantle with red cross.

Hiram Abiff's immortality lies not in the eternal existence of his soul in some heavenly kingdom, but in the minds and bodies of those Masters who came after him, men charged to take his place and to finish what the mythical Grand Master had begun. Their duty was to make the plans and direct the "workmen," the Entrants and Fellows of the Craft, in achieving Abiff's goal, the completion of the Temple of Solomon.

All this has only the vaguest connection with the biblical account. According to scripture, Hiram was not an architect but a master worker in brass and bronze. He was not murdered but lived to see the temple completed and then went back to his home. The clues to Masonic origin and purpose are found in the allegorical legend, not in the scriptures.

As we search British history to find an unfinished temple as a basis for an exclusively British secret society, we find just one answer, in the religious order that often called itself by that simple name alone: the Temple. Jacques de Molay and his predecessors signed documents over the title *Magister Templi*, Master of the Temple. And *that* temple, taking its name from the Temple of Solomon, certainly was left unfinished upon the murder of its masters, who also had been tortured to reveal their secrets by three assassins who ultimately destroyed them. Not Jubela, Jubelo, and Jubelum, but Philip the Fair of France, Pope Clement V, and the order of the Knights of the Hospital of St. John of Jerusalem. Many who have read only the Catholic Church's summations of the Templar suppression may object, stating that only the king of France could be considered the "assassin" of the Knights Templar, having done all of the dirty work and having coerced a weak pope to help him. True, that is the church's usual version to this very day, but the historical facts speak somewhat to the contrary....

When Edward II of England declined to torture the Templars, the pope could have thrown the problem back to Edward's father-in-law, the king of France: No one forced Clement V to dispatch ten church torture specialists to London. The pope could have lived with the acquittal of the Templars on Cyprus: No one forced him to demand a new trial, or to dispatch a torture team with the power to draw upon the local Dominicans and Franciscans if extra help was required.

> The legend of Hiram Abiff tells us that it is not a coincidence that two organizations found their central identification in the Temple of Solomon, because one group gave birth to the other.

Nor did the king of France prevail in his desire that one of his family be made the head of a combined Hospitaller/Templar order, with full access to their combined wealth. And if Clement V had been merely a timorous puppet pope with Philip pulling the strings, as church historians would have us believe, the kings of France would have been the new owners of the Templar properties in France, not the Hospitallers. The pope was much tougher, or at least much more obstinate, than we have been led to believe and it would appear that he had contrived a plan of his own in concert with the Hospitallers.

That order has managed to escape any criticism in the matter of the Templar suppression, but apparently only because it had kept a low profile throughout, probably for the very good reason that its role and its rewards had been worked out in advance. It is well known that the papacy was in favor of a union of the Templars and Hospitallers and had already determined that Foulques de Villaret, master of the Hospitallers, would be the Grand Master of the combined orders. The Templars, at their headquarters on Cyprus, had heard of the serious intent to combine the orders and had taken the time to prepare a written rebuttal. The Hospitallers, at their own headquarters on that same island, must have received the same information, yet they prepared no rebuttal, written or verbal. In fact, de Villaret managed to stay away from the meeting in France altogether, with no recorded papal criticism for his absence. That was undoubtedly because his presence wasn't needed and because there was no point in chancing a confrontation between the two orders, especially since the pope was already dedicated to looking after the interests of the Hospitallers. Not only did the Hospitallers offer no objection to the concept of the merger, but they made no attempt whatever to speak up for their brother warrior-monks as they were arrested and tortured. They simply stayed out of it and bided their time, until Clement V, much to the anger of King Philip, declared that all of the confiscated Templar property would go to the Knights Hospitaller and that all released Templars could be taken into the Hospitaller order, thereby achieving *de facto* the union he had been planning all along, with full Hospitaller approval and cooperation. If one looks for motive, the Hospitaller order was the major beneficiary of the suppression of the Templars, as had probably been planned from the beginning. The pope and the

Hospitallers together thwarted the aims of Philip of France, and there should be no doubt that the Hospitallers rank as one of the three assassins of the Order of the Temple.

An interesting point about the legend of Hiram Abiff is that in it, the three assassins have already been punished, have been "brought to the Jubé." Certainly there were wars with France before and after the Templar suppression, and it becomes increasingly probable that the punishments meted out to the Hospitallers during the Peasant's Rebellion, including the murder of their prior, were acts of vengeance carried out under the cover of a political disturbance. As for punishment of the Holy See, the Templar-spawned underground movement was probably the most effective enemy the church had in the British Isles before, during, and after the Reformation. Over five hundred years after the Templar suppression, popes were still condemning Freemasonry for welcoming members of all religious faiths and for failing to acknowledge Roman Catholicism as the one true church. In Secret Masonry, religious dissenters and protesters had an organization that would help them, hide them, and provide communication with others of their kind, and as the years went by, conflicts between popes and kings, between popes and the people, and between popes and their own priests provided a river of recruits for a secret society that permitted them to worship God in their own ways. All three assassins of the Order of the Temple had reason to regret their actions against the bearded knights.

A major mystery of the Legend of Hiram Abiff is the identity of "that which was lost." Some Masonic historians take the allegory literally, almost always a mistake, and state that what was lost was the "word" of the Grand Master, or the "secrets" of the Master. What the Templars had lost, literally, was their wealth, respect, and power. What the allegory suggests was lost was the architect, the planner who was needed to finish the temple and provide the leadership to move forward. The man being initiated as a Master by acting out the murder is being turned into another Hiram. Every Master takes that role, and *becomes* Hiram (a name by which Masons sometimes address each other). He is the "son of the widow," and it is *his* task to replace that which was lost: the leadership, the direction, the work required to "finish" the building of the (Order of the) Temple, which was brutally stopped by beatings and murder. Now, of course, that leadership, that elevation to the role of one of the supreme leaders of the society, has been changed. Every Mason has the opportunity to become a Master, and the initiate may be somewhat confused that what appears to him to be just another degree on his ladder of progress in Masonry should be so emphatic about the means of seeking and providing help, and so empathic about the need to guard his brother Master Masons' secrets.

The symbolism born of allegory was accepted as factual.

In summary, the legend of Hiram Abiff tells us that it is not a coincidence that two organizations found their central identification in the Temple of Solomon, because one group gave birth to the other. It explains the purpose of the successor group, the Freemasons, by recounting, allegorically, the fate of the prior group, the Order of the Temple. The temple was left unfinished because of the murder of the Grand Master. The man being exposed to this legend in his initiation takes the role of the Grand Master and then assumes his task, the completion of the Temple. In this sense,

the Freemason is neither an "operative" mason with tools in his hands nor a "speculative" mason who joins a guild of masons as a nonworking member. Rather, he is a *symbolic* mason, whose building task is not connected to any actual building but is concerned only with the survival and growth of the symbolic temple, the Order of the Poor Fellow-Soldiers of Christ and the Temple of Solomon: the Knights Templar.

As the true origins of Masonry were obscured by time and then lost altogether, the Freemasons were left with the allegory only, and they created a fantasy world by accepting that allegory as factual. One Masonic writer was awestruck that Masonry had preserved for over two thousand years these details of the building of the Temple of Solomon which had escaped the authors of the Old Testament. The legend of Hiram Abiff was taught not as legend but a recitation of historical fact.

Along with the acceptance of Hiram Abiff as a real person, Freemasonry for generations taught that the order had been founded among the workmen who built the Temple of Solomon. That building became a focal point for Masonic reverence and respect. Artists' renderings of Solomon's temple came to decorate the walls of Masonic temples, and some Masons made pilgrimages to the site. Some managed to bring back to their lodges a piece of stone from the Temple Mount or from nearby quarries, relics that were displayed proudly with all of the aura of religious relics. Even today, long after Masonry shifted its claims of origin from the construction of the temple to the medieval guilds of stonemasons, there are Masons firmly convinced that their order began in the building of that temple.

Finally more sober minds did prevail, and Masonry did come to acknowledge that the story of Hiram Abiff was not factual but was an important piece of Masonic mythology. Its acceptance as fact had caused the whole fraternity to bend in the direction of the building trades and had led them to identify every common stonemason's tool as a Masonic symbol, to identify the Supreme Being as the Great Architect of the Universe, to teach that Masons had built the great Gothic cathedrals, and to include details of architecture and building in the Masonic rituals.

Now that the story of Hiram Abiff has been recognized as legend, not fact, all of the building-trade symbolism generated by the literal acceptance of the story remains, and that symbolism serves to confuse origins and purposes because it has become imbued with a reality and antiquity it does not have. In the absence of written records, centuries of time played their inevitable role of obscuring beginnings and purposes, and the rush to embrace the building trades built a screen few cared to look behind. The symbolism born of allegory was accepted as factual.

The mystery is simply this: If the story of Hiram Abiff and the Masonic role in the building of Solomon's temple are acknowledged as myths, how did that temple become central to Masonic ritual and legend? Certainly medieval stonemasons provide no answer to that question, and as the medieval guild theory itself falls away, there appears to be no answer to that mystery...except one. The temple that is so honored and revered by Freemasonry is not a building but is the only other order that ever identified itself with that building: the Knights of the Temple.

The Wayfarer *by John J. Robinson*

The principal purpose of this discourse is to call attention to a field of research so far untouched by Masonic scholars: the evidence to be found in the work of artists of the Middle Ages. Given that a secret society did exist in medieval Britain, it would be much simpler for an artist to conceal its symbolism and allegory in his paintings than for a chronicler to attempt to conceal them in his writings.

The painting reproduced [here] is an outstanding example of the possibilities. It is *The Wayfarer*, by the Flemish artist Hieronymus Bosch. Those familiar with Bosch's work have come to expect graphic portrayals of a wide range of hideous, distorted demons. *The Wayfarer* is different in that it depicts no demons or monsters, although it is packed with symbolism, much of it Masonic in nature.

Take a good look at the painting. The wayfarer has his left trouser leg pushed up to the knee. It might be pointed out that the trouser leg is up to accommodate a bandage, but no minor calf wound requires a slipper on one foot, with a shoe on the other.

The straps of the wayfarer's backpack are not over his shoulder, where they belong. Instead, Bosch has put a strap around his upper arms, binding him like a Masonic cable-tow. The feather we might expect to find in his hat is not there. Bosch has replaced it with a plumb bob, another Masonic symbol.

Why is the man carrying his hat in his hand, rather than conveniently wearing it on his head? Bosch may have wanted his hood ready to pull down over his face to "hoodwink" him, a word that suggests that this is the way a man was blindfolded in ancient Masonic initiation. It was a common practice at the time and was incorporated into the language for future ages in the expression "to pull the wool over his eyes."

Ahead of the traveler is a gate with a strange brace. Everyone who knows anything about wooden farm gates knows that the brace goes from one corner to the diagonally opposed corner, creating immovable triangles. The brace on Bosch's gate rises above the top rail, then comes back down to the corner. This produces a craftsman's square on top of the gate.

Now consider the painting as a whole. The traveling man is moving from left to right, or from west to east, leaving behind him a rude, crude world. A serving maid lounges in the doorway of a decrepit tavern, holding a pitcher, while a customer kisses her, holding his hand on her breast. Around the corner, a man is urinating against the wall. In the courtyard, pigs feed at a trough, while an angry dog with a spiked collar crouches, deciding whether or not to attack.

The Prodigal Son. Hieronymus Bosch (c. 1450–1516). *Photo: Kavaler / Art Resource, NY Museum Boymans van Beuningen, Rotterdam, The Netherlands.*

With a few more steps the wayfarer will pass through the gate of the square and enter a land of peace and plenty, as symbolized by the placid milk cow. In the tree above his head is perched an owl, the medieval symbol for wisdom.

The final question is one of motivation. To have known the Masonic symbols before 1717 (if indeed they existed in his time), Bosch would have to have been a Masonic initiate. Is it likely that the artist would have been attracted to, and invited into, a secret society dedicated to protecting religious dissidents from the wrath of the Church? It is very probable. Bosch is known to have been a member of a religious fraternity frowned upon by the Church. His cynical portrayals of drunken, carousing monks and nuns indicate a man angry at the Church, especially in view of several condemnations of his work as heretical.

It is possible, of course, that the Masonic symbols in this painting are all merely coincidences. If so, this is the most incredible collection of Masonic coincidences that we may ever expect to see assembled in a single work. If, however, the symbols are not there coincidentally, then this painting provides the very first graphic evidence of the existence of Masonic symbolism about five hundred years ago, in the late fifteenth century.

The Knights Templar and the Secret of the Scroll   by John White

John White is an author in the fields of consciousness research and higher human development. He has published fifteen books, including The Meeting of Science and Spirit *and* What Is Enlightenment? *He is a 32nd Degree Mason of the Scottish Rite and a Knight Templar of the York Rite. He lives in Cheshire, Connecticut.*

Dan Brown's new book, *The Lost Symbol*, depicts Freemasonry as having a fundamental role in the founding of America. The "lost" symbol or final secret of Freemasonry is used by Brown in a fast-paced thriller which, along the way, gives very good information about Masonic lore and its role in the formation of our nation. (I say that as a Mason.) Images of light are central to it all, and during Masonic initiations, the answer which a candidate gives to the question, "What do you desire most of all?" is "More light." To put it plainly, light means knowledge or, more properly, wisdom. The purpose of Freemasonry is to "make good men better" by imparting ethical teachings and esoteric knowledge which, when deeply understood, impart wisdom. The tradition of Freemasonry speaks of the "Lost Word," which its legendary founder, Hiram Abiff, took with him to the grave as he was building the Temple of Solomon in Jerusalem about 1,000 B.C. Is there a secret knowledge embedded in Freemasonry which has become "lost" or "invisible" to it? Various Masonic writers have indicated that is precisely the case. Freemasonry, they say, has lost touch with the deeper wisdom of its tradition. Some of its rituals seem to obliquely refer to that original-but-lost knowledge. For example, in "Royal Arch Masonry"[1] by W. L. Tucker, we read:

> We are told of the return of the sojourners [Jews in exile in Babylon] who wanted to assist in the rebuilding of the Temple and we are told of the Vault. This is pure history. After the candidate is lowered into the Vault [in the modern Scottish Rite ceremony reenacting the history], he feels around until he finds something like a scroll of vellum or parchment, part of the long-lost Sacred Law. What

was found really was a way to return to the way of life founded on the principles of the Bible, symbolized by the scroll which was found.

In the last decade or so, a growing number of Masonic scholars and historians have discussed a topic that may link directly to Tucker's statement above. In brief: There is evidence suggesting that a secret vault beneath the floor of Rosslyn Chapel near Edinburgh, Scotland, may hold some long-lost scrolls once possessed by the Knights Templar. (Rosslyn Chapel's floor plan replicates a section of the Temple of Solomon; Rosslyn Castle and environs, under the Earl of Sinclair, allegedly became the headquarters of the Knights Templar after they fled arrest in France in 1307, when King Philip IV violently suppressed the Templars.) According to this emerging view of the Order of the Temple, or Templary, those scrolls, purportedly copper, were obtained by the very first Templars in the twelfth century when they were allowed by the King of Jerusalem to establish their headquarters on the site of the Temple of Solomon. Working stealthily to excavate a secret vault beneath the Temple, they obtained a great hidden treasure which they knew to be there;

that apparently was the true reason for their presence in Jerusalem. Part of the treasure may have been actual gold and jewels; that would help to account for the meteoric rise in wealth which the Templars are known to have achieved. But the greatest treasure, it is believed, would have been the scrolls containing ancient esoteric knowledge about the secret of Jesus and the Bible.

What is that secret knowledge? In a word: enlightenment. I do not mean simply psychological transformation of the mind, but rather psychophysical transformation or transubstantiation of flesh, blood and bone into a body of light—precisely the resurrection body which Jesus Christ demonstrated in his conquest of death. That is the "way to return to the way of life founded on the principles of the Bible," which Tucker mentions above. It would certainly qualify as "the rediscovery of the lost Master's Word in the rubble of Solomon's temple" noted by Thomas C. Berry in a 2001 letter to the editor of *Royal Arch Mason*.[2]

On the basis of my reason, research, and personal experience, I have concluded that the real secret of pharaonic Egypt, from which so much in Freemasonry purportedly derives, is the attainment of the light body.

That, I think, is the highest teaching that was conferred on initiates in the King's Chamber of the Great Pyramid. I also think that esoteric knowledge was brought by Moses from Egypt into Judaism and later was recorded on the copper scrolls presumably hidden beneath the Temple in Jerusalem. (Moses, a Hebrew, was adopted as a baby by the Pharaoh's daughter and was raised as royalty, so he would have been schooled in the spiritual practices of Egypt.) So if the Templars recovered that hidden teaching, it would be the greatest treasure in the world, far more so than gold and jewels. It would be the secret of immortality and what Freemasonry calls "the lodge on high not made with human hands." I can't help but wonder if those scrolls are now buried beneath the floor of Rosslyn Chapel, as the recent book *The Hiram Key* indicates. If this speculation is correct, the greatest and most valuable aspect of the Templar treasure would be a Codex of Enlightenment.

There is another aspect to the newly emerging story of the Knights Templar which also excites me. It is the possibility that America is the result of a Templar/ Masonic experiment intended to create the New Israel or Promised Land in the New World—not a Jewish nation but a universally God-centered and moral society, as Israel was called to be by Jesus and, earlier, by the prophets. Here's my thinking about it, which I admit is highly speculative.

Several recent books about the Knights Templar and the Holy Grail indicate that the African kingdom of Mali should be credited with two momentous facts bearing profoundly on Euro-American history. According to Michael Bradley in his 1988 book *Holy Grail Across the Atlantic* and, building on that, William F. Mann's 1999 *The Labyrinth of the Grail*, by the fourteenth century, the Emperor of Mali had ships going to the New World, and other Africans had crossed much earlier. Stone statues in Central America of men with negroid features appear to be mute testimony to this extraordinary achievement. Transatlantic travel could not have been done without the development of a method to measure longitude. That means Africans solved the problem of determining longitude at sea long before Europeans did. However, the knowledge was lost and apparently had no influence on the solution developed by Europeans in the eighteenth century.

Why it was lost and why Malian seafaring culture declined are topics

Burning of the Grand Master of the Templars, 1314 (c.1375–1400). Jacques de Molay, last grand master of the Knights Templar is burnt at the stake with Geoffroi de Charney, Preceptor of Normandy. From the "Chroniques de France ou de St Denis." *British Library, London Great Britain. HIP / Art Resource, NY.*

for research. The Bradley-Mann thesis contends that knowledge of longitude measurement was passed from Mali to Arabic culture, and thence to the Knights Templar, whose interactions with Arab Muslims in the Middle East were sometimes friendly rather than hostile. The Knights Templar, in turn, kept that knowledge secret, using it for their own purposes.

Those purposes may have included voyages to the New World a full century or more before Columbus, through Prince Henry Sinclair of Scotland and Orkney. In 1398 he sent a three-ship expedition which reached Nova Scotia and the East Coast of America, where the remains of a buried Scottish knight at Westford, Massachusetts, and the so-called Viking Tower at Newport, Rhode Island, indicate the presence of the Sinclair expedition. The Westford site has a knight carved into a rock ledge where the remnant of what appears to be a broken ancient sword was found. The knight's shield bears the crest of Clan Gunn, who were subjects of Sinclair. The Viking Tower's interior geometry, the researchers say, is reflective of Templar design and fourteenth-century Scotland rather than Viking architecture.

Sinclair's forebears had granted refuge in Scotland to fugitive Knights

> Because of their experience with the political corruption of the Old World, the Templars apparently conceived a secret plan for creating a new and better society in the North American wilderness.

Templar when King Philip of France disbanded the Order of the Temple in 1307 and burned its Grand Master, Jacques de Molay, at the stake. The Templar fugitives' fleet of ships left La Rochelle, France, and sailed around Ireland to Scotland. Those Knights Templar made Rosslyn Castle, the ancestral home of the Sinclairs, their center of operations. Rosslyn Chapel was begun in the mid-1400s and completed before the end of that century. It contains carvings of maize (Indian corn) and aloe, plants which are native to the New World. (Also see *The Lost Treasure of the Knights Templar* by Steven Sora.)

How did the builders of Rosslyn Chapel get knowledge of New World plants a century before Columbus discovered America? As I mentioned above, the Templar contact with Mali-Arab culture during the crusades led to it.

Because of their experience with the political corruption of the Old World, the Templars apparently conceived a secret plan for creating a new and better society in the North American wilderness. That plan became the basis of Freemasonry and its influence over the founding of America. Francis Bacon, who was a driving force behind the creation of the Royal Society for scientific research, was connected to the Templar remnant. He also wrote *The New Atlantis* about a mythical land to the west, and his account of that land shows remarkable parallels to later historical developments in the New World, as if his book were a kind of secret blueprint for Masonic endeavors in the vast and virgin continent.

Over several centuries, according to the new view, Templary was transformed into Freemasonry, and by the time of the American Revolution, many of the Founders of America—those who fought for the nation, those who signed the Declaration of Independence and those who created the Constitution—were Masons. Among them were George Washington, Benjamin Franklin, John Adams, John Hancock, Paul Revere, John Paul Jones, and many others.

Perhaps, just perhaps, there is a secret history to America, much like what has been alleged by Manly Palmer Hall in *America's Secret Destiny* and by others who claim there is an occult or esoteric foundation to America. Perhaps, just perhaps, America is in part a Templar/Masonic effort to advance human society on the basis of secret knowledge and secret activities, much as fables about the Illuminati claim. (Please note: I refer to the true Illuminati, better known as Ascended Masters, whose native state is the resurrection body or light body and who constitute the "lodge on high not made with human hands." The Illuminati conspiracy launched in 1776 by Adam Weishaupt of Bavaria was a false and corrupt use of the term which was rightly denounced by true Masons.)

It's all far from being clear and certain to me, but if there is anything sacred about America, it is the idea that God is the author of our being and the source of our freedom, our sovereignty, our rights, our justice and our human dignity. Those are very Masonic ideas, injected into the social-political institutions of our nation by those great Masons who were among the creators of America. Was it purely chance, or has the hidden hand of God been guiding our affairs through the centuries and working through barely visible means which carry the symbols and substance of Freemasonry?

FINDING THE LOST SYMBOLS IN WASHINGTON, D.C.

Above, the Capitol dome. Right, view of *The Apotheosis of Washington* inside the dome.

The Capitol

The Capitol as it looked in 1800 to the artist William Russell Birch.

After George Washington laid the cornerstone of the Capitol on September 18, 1793, work proceeded slowly. One of the architects modified the design without authorization, which resulted in his dismissal. The superintendent of construction resigned in 1798. Only the Senate wing was near completion when the Senate, House of Representatives, Supreme Court, district courts, and Library of Congress moved into it in November 1800.

In 1803, Benjamin Henry Latrobe became superintendent of construction and attempted to persuade President Jefferson to approve significant changes, criticizing both the Capitol's original design and its execution. Latrobe was

Perspective from the Northeast.

compelled to continue working with the established plan, and the scene imagined in his 1806 watercolor *Perspective from the Northeast* never came to pass.

The Capitol still did not have a dome when Washington was attacked by the British during the War of 1812. The building was set afire and badly damaged.

Latrobe was appointed Architect of the Capitol in 1815 and given the opportunity of rebuilding it. He was now permitted to promote his own design, which was submitted in 1817.

Charles Bulfinch became Architect of the Capitol in 1818 and followed through with many of Latrobe's ideas. Much of the building was complete by 1829. Bulfinch was the designer of the wood-framed green copper dome seen in this print by E. Sasche & Co. from 1852.

Also seen in this print are the extensions to the Senate and House wings built in the 1850s by Thomas Walter. The building now seemed to plead for a taller dome. Construction on Walter's design for a new, cast-iron dome began in 1855 and the work was still in progress during Abraham Lincoln's inauguration in 1861.

U.S. Capitol after burning by the British on August 24, 1814. Watercolor by George Munger.

When Constantino Brumidi put the final touches on his fresco *The Apotheosis of Washington* in 1866, the dome we see today was complete.

Lincoln's first inauguration, March 4, 1861.

Apotheosis of Washington

The Apotheosis of Washington in the eye of the Rotunda of the U.S. Capitol was painted in the true fresco technique by Constantino Brumidi in 1865. Brumidi (1805–1880) was born and trained in Rome and had painted in the Vatican and Roman palaces before immigrating to the United States in 1852. A master of creating three-dimensional forms and figures on flat walls, Brumidi painted frescoes and murals throughout the Capitol from 1855 until his death. The canopy fresco, his most ambitious work at the Capitol, was painted at the end of the Civil War, soon after the new dome was completed. Suspended 180 above the Rotunda floor, it covers an area of 4,664 square feet. The figures, up to 15 feet tall, were painted to be intelligible from close up as well as from 180 feet below. Some of the groups and figures were inspired by classical and Renaissance images, especially those by Italian master Raphael.

In the central group of the fresco, Brumidi depicted George Washington rising to the heavens in glory, flanked by female figures representing Liberty and Victory/Fame. A rainbow arches at his feet, and thirteen maidens symbolizing the original states flank the three central figures. (The word *apotheosis* means the raising of a person to the rank of a god, or the glorification of a person as an ideal.)

The Apotheosis of Washington

Six groups of figures line the perimeter of the canopy; the following list begins below the central group and proceeds clockwise:

- **War,** with Armed Freedom and the eagle defeating Tyranny and Kingly Power
- **Science,** with Minerva teaching Benjamin Franklin, Robert Fulton, and Samuel F.B. Morse
- **Marine,** with Neptune holding his trident and Venus holding the transatlantic cable, which was being laid at the time the fresco was painted
- **Commerce,** with Mercury handing a bag of money to Robert Morris, financier of the American Revolution
- **Mechanics,** with Vulcan at the anvil and forge, producing a cannon and a steam engine
- **Agriculture,** with Ceres seated on the McCormick Reaper, accompanied by America in a red liberty cap and Flora picking flowers

Horatio Greenough's statue of Washington, modeled after a depiction of Zeus from ancient Greece, was intended for the original rotunda of the Capitol and arrived there in 1841. With Washington clad in something like a toga, it ignited controversy and ridicule, and was soon banished to the lawn on the east side of the Capitol building.

At one point it seemed to hail the completion of the new dome.

And it apparently played a featured role for the crowd at the inauguration of Rutherford B. Hayes in 1877.

The deification of Washington had begun immediately after his death, which had truly shaken the nation.

His image was everywhere. Schoolchildren were taught to admire his character. High above the other Founders, Washington was beyond reproach.

The fate of Greenough's statue provides something of a counterpoint to the reverential treatment of Washington's memory usually accorded by the American people. Today the statue occupies a small foyer on the second floor of the National Museum of American History.

The National Statuary Hall

The concept of a National Statuary Hall originated in the middle of the nineteenth century, even before the completion of the present House wing in 1857. At that time, the House of Representatives moved into its new larger chamber and the old vacant chamber became a thoroughfare between the Rotunda and the House wing. Suggestions for the use of the chamber were made as early as 1853.

The entire collection now consists of one hundred statues contributed by the fifty states.

For a list of the 100 statues, please visit the website of the office of the Architect of the Capitol.

Statue of Freedom

The Statue of Freedom by Thomas Crawford is the crowning feature of the dome of the United States Capitol. The bronze statue is a classical female figure of Freedom wearing flowing draperies. Her right hand rests upon the hilt of a sheathed sword; her left holds a laurel wreath of victory and the shield of the United States with thirteen stripes. Her helmet is encircled by stars and features a crest composed of an eagle's head, feathers, and talons, a reference to the costume of Native Americans. A brooch inscribed "U.S." secures her fringed robes. She stands on a cast-iron globe encircled with the words *E Pluribus Unum*, then the national motto. The lower part of the base is decorated with fasces and wreaths. Ten bronze points tipped with platinum are attached to her headdress, shoulders, and shield for protection from lightning. The bronze statue stands 19 feet 6 inches tall and weighs approximately 15,000 pounds. Her crest rises 288 feet above the east front plaza.

A monumental statue for the top of the national Capitol appeared in Architect Thomas U. Walter's original drawing for the new cast-iron dome, which was authorized in 1855. Walter's drawing showed the outline of a statue representing Liberty; Crawford proposed an allegorical figure of "Freedom triumphant in War and Peace." After Secretary of War Jefferson Davis objected to the sculptor's intention to include a liberty cap, the symbol of freed slaves, Crawford replaced it with a crested Roman helmet.

Crawford was commissioned to design the Statue of Freedom in 1855 and executed the plaster model for the statue in his studio in Rome. He died in 1857 before the model left his studio.

Beginning in 1860, the statue was cast in five main sections by Clark Mills, whose bronze foundry was located on the outskirts of Washington. Work was halted in 1861 because of the Civil War, but by the end of 1862 the statue was finished and temporarily displayed on the Capitol grounds. The cost of the statue, exclusive of installation, was $23,796.82.

Late in 1863, construction of the dome was sufficiently advanced for the installation of the statue, which was hoisted in sections and assembled atop the cast-iron pedestal. The final section, the figure's head and shoulders, was raised on December 2, 1863, to a salute of 35 guns answered by the guns of the 12 forts around Washington.

CHAPTER TWO
America's Secret Destiny

"Would that I could paint his mind."

–Nicholas Hilliard, who painted a miniature cameo of Bacon

Francis Bacon, Viscount St. Alban, 1641.
William Marshall. © National Portrait Gallery, London.

Excerpt from The New Atlantis *by Sir Francis Bacon*

Sir Francis Bacon is suspected of everything—from inventing modern science to writing Shakespeare and the King James Bible (into which he inserted numerous Baconian ciphers). According to some, he even designed a wonderful experiment: America.

Seeking refuge, Langdon and Katherine Solomon run past the Folger Shakespeare Library, which Langdon thinks seems to offer "appropriate camouflage for them tonight, as it housed the original Latin manuscript of Francis Bacon's New Atlantis, *the utopian vision on which the American forefathers had allegedly modeled a new world based on ancient knowledge."*

First published in 1627, one year after Bacon's death, The New Atlantis *is a utopian fable in which desperate sailors discover an island whose inhabitants minister to them, and recount a history of the world that the Europeans have lost or forgotten. Their ideal society centers around a college, of sorts, which is called "Salomon's House." There, "The end of our foundation is the knowledge of causes, and secret motions of things; and the enlarging of the bounds of human empire, the effecting of all things possible."*

Francis Bacon, Viscount St. Alban, 1731?
John Vanderbank. © National Portrait Gallery, London.

In this excerpt the Governor of the island responds to questions from the sailors:

"So as marvel you not at the thin population of America, nor at the rudeness and ignorance of the people; for you must account your inhabitants of America as a young people; younger a thousand years, at the least, than the rest of the world: for that there was so much time between the universal flood and their particular inundation. For the poor remnant of human seed, which remained in their mountains, peopled the country again slowly, by little and little; and being simple and savage people (not like Noah and his sons, which was the chief family of the earth); they were not able to leave letters, arts, and civility to their posterity; and having likewise in their mountainous habitations been used (in respect of the extreme cold of those regions) to clothe themselves with the skins of tigers, bears, and great hairy goats, that they have in those parts; when after they came down into the valley, and found the intolerable heats which are there, and knew no means of lighter apparel, they were forced to begin the custom of going naked, which continueth at this day.

Only they take great pride and delight in the feathers of birds; and this also they took from those their ancestors of the mountains, who were invited unto it by the infinite flights of birds that came up to the high grounds, while the waters stood below. So you see, by this main accident of time, we lost our traffic with the Americans, with whom of, all others, in regard they lay nearest to us, we had most commerce.

"As for the other parts of the world, it is most manifest that in the ages following (whether it were in respect of wars, or by a natural revolution of time), navigation did every where greatly decay; and specially far voyages (the rather by the use of galleys, and such vessels as could hardly brook the ocean) were altogether left and omitted. So then, that part of intercourse which could be from other nations to sail to us, you see how it hath long since ceased; except it were by some rare accident, as this of yours. But now of the cessation of that other part of intercourse, which might be by our sailing to other nations, I must yield you some other cause. For I cannot say (if I shall say truly), but our shipping, for number, strength, mariners, pilots, and all things that appertain to navigation, is as great as ever; and therefore why we should sit at home, I shall now give you an account by itself: and it will draw nearer to give you satisfaction to your principal question.

"There reigned in this land, about nineteen hundred years ago, a king, whose memory of all others we most adore; not superstitiously, but as a divine instrument, though a mortal man; his name was Solamona: and we esteem him as the lawgiver of our nation. This king had a large heart, inscrutable for good; and was wholly bent to make his kingdom and people happy. He therefore, taking into consideration how sufficient and substantive this land was to maintain itself without any aid (at all) of the foreigner; being five thousand six hundred miles in circuit, and of rare fertility of soil in the greatest part thereof; and finding also the shipping of this country might be plentifully set on work, both by fishing and by transportations from port to port, and likewise by sailing unto some small islands that are not far from us, and are under the crown and laws of this state; and, recalling into his memory the happy and flourishing estate wherein this land then was; so as it might be a thousand ways altered to the worse, but scarce any one way to the better; though nothing wanted to his noble and heroical intentions, but only (as far as human foresight might reach) to give perpetuity to that which was in his time so happily established. Therefore amongst his other fundamental laws of this kingdom, he did ordain the interdicts and prohibitions which we have touching entrance of strangers; which at that

> "We maintain a trade not for gold, silver, or jewels; nor for silks; nor for spices; nor any other commodity of matter; but only for God's first creature, which was Light…"

write it as it is spoken. So as I take it to be denominate of the king of the Hebrews, which is famous with you, and no stranger to us. For we have some parts of his works, which with you are lost; namely, that natural history, which he wrote, of all plants, from the cedar of Libanus to the moss that groweth out of

time (though it was after the calamity of America) was frequent; doubting novelties, and commixture of manners.…

"And here I shall seem a little to digress, but you will by and by find it pertinent. Ye shall understand (my dear friends) that amongst the excellent acts of that king, one above all hath the pre-eminence. It was the erection and institution of an Order or Society, which we call Salomon's House; the noblest foundation (as we think) that ever was upon the earth; and the lanthorn of this kingdom. It is dedicated to the study of the works and creatures of God. Some think it beareth the founder's name a little corrupted, as if it should be Solamona's House. But the records

the wall, and of all things that have life and motion. This maketh me think that our king, finding himself to symbolize in many things with that king of the Hebrews (which lived many years before him), honored him with the title of this foundation. And I am rather induced to be of this opinion, for that I find in ancient records this Order or Society is sometimes called Salomon's House, and sometimes the College of the Six Days Works; whereby I am satisfied that our excellent king had learned from the Hebrews that God had created the world and all that therein is within six days: and therefore he instituting that House for the finding out of the true nature of all things (whereby God might have the more glory in the workmanship of them, and insert the more fruit in the use of them), did give it also that second name.

"But now to come to our present purpose. When the king had forbidden to all his people navigation into any part that was not under his crown, he made nevertheless this ordinance; that every twelve years there should be set forth, out of this kingdom two ships, appointed to several voyages; that in either of these ships there should be a mission of three of the Fellows or Brethren of Salomon's House; whose errand was only to give us knowledge of the affairs and state of those countries to which they were designed, and especially of the sciences, arts, manufactures, and inventions of all the world; and withal to bring unto us books, instruments, and patterns in every kind: That the ships, after they had landed the brethren, should return; and that the brethren should stay abroad till the new mission. These ships are not otherwise fraught, than with store of victuals, and good quantity of treasure to remain with the brethren, for the buying of such things and rewarding of such persons as they should think fit. Now for me to tell you how the vulgar sort of mariners are contained from being discovered at land; and how they that must be put on shore for any time, color themselves under the names of other nations; and to what places these voyages have been designed; and what places of rendezvous are appointed for the new missions; and the like circumstances of the practique; I may not do it: neither is it much to your desire. But thus you see we maintain a trade not for gold, silver, or jewels; nor for silks; nor for spices; nor any other commodity of matter; but only for God's first creature, which was Light: to have light (I say) of the growth of all parts of the world."

The Invisible College—On Wheels!

by Frances A. Yates

Dame Frances Yates is unable to turn up any evidence—despite their hugely influential manifestos—that an actual fraternal organization of Rosicrucians existed during the seventeenth century!

She urges "sensible people and sensible historians" to think of Rosicrucianism instead as "a certain style of thinking which is historically recognizable without raising the question of whether a Rosicrucian style of thinker belonged to a secret society."

Since no one could find the R.C. Brothers to join, they were referred to as "the Invisibles."

This print shows a peculiar building above which is an inscription containing the words *Collegium Fraternitatis* and Fama, and is dated 1618. On the building, on either side of its door, there is a rose and a cross. We are therefore presumably now beholding a representation of the Invisible College of the R.C. Brothers. Another main Rosicrucian emblem is alluded to in the wings with Jehova's Name, expressive of the words which seal the conclusion of the Fama, "Under the shadow of thy wings, Jehova."

In the sky, to left and right of the central Name and wings, are a Serpent and a Swan, bearing stars and alluding to the "new stars" in Serpentarius and Cygnus mentioned in the Confessio as prophetic of a new dispensation.

A hand proceeding from a cloud around the Name holds the building, as on a thread, and the building itself is winged, and on wheels. Does this mean that the winged, moveable College of the Fraternity of the Rosy Cross is Nowhere, like Utopia, invisible, because non-existent in a literal sense? The Rose Cross College is defended by three figures on its battlements who bear shields on which are engraved the Name, and brandish what appear to be feathers. Are they angelic presences defending those dwelling under the Shadow of the Wings?

From one side of the building projects a trumpet, and the initials "C.R.F.," perhaps "Christian Rosencreutz Frater," announced by the trumpeting of the manifestos. On the other side, a hand holding a sword projects, labelled "Jul. de Campi," alluding to the character

The Invisible College of the Rose Cross Fraternity. From Theophilus Schweighardt, *Speculum Sophicum Rhodo-Stauroticum.* © Adam McLean 2002.

called "Julianus de Campis" who appears in the Speculum and whose defence of the R.C. Brotherhood was printed with the 1616 (Cassel) edition of the manifestos. Perhaps this is why he brandishes a defensive sword in the print. Near the projecting arm, the words "Jesus nobis omnia" are written on the building, a motto which also occurs in the Fama and is expressive of the point already quoted from the Speculum, that the true approach to the macro-micro-cosmical mystery is in the imitation of Christ as defined by Thomas à Kempis. Other little pairs of wings have inscriptions, one is "T.S.," perhaps Theophilus Schweighardt, the supposed author of the Speculum.

A figure kneeling on the ground on the right directs most earnest prayers upwards to the Name. Seen within the windows of the angel-protected College of the Rose Cross Fraternity are figures of people who appear to be engaged in studies. A man is working at something at one window, at the other there appear to be scientific instruments of some kind. The prayerful attitude of the kneeling figure might be expressive of an approach to scientific, angelic, and divine studies rather like that of John Dee.

I leave the reader to puzzle further over the mysteries of this print which is undoubtedly showing us in emblematic form the message of the Rosicrucian Fama. We are here near the center of the "joke," the ludibrium, in the minds of the strange people who framed the Rosicrucian manifestos.

> A hand proceeding from a cloud around the Name holds the building, as on a thread, and the building itself is winged, and on wheels.

Dame Frances Amelia Yates DBE was the author of The Rosicrucian Enlightenment *(from which this excerpt is drawn),* Giordano Bruno and the Hermetic Tradition, *and* The Art of Memory.

Masonic Civility During the Revolutionary War *by Michael Baigent and Richard Leigh*

Freemasonry (at the time of the Revolutionary War) was a repository for an imaginatively stirring and potent idealism, which it was able, in a fashion uniquely its own, to disseminate. Most colonists did not actually read Locke, Hume, Voltaire, Diderot, or Rousseau, any more than most British soldiers did. Through the lodges, however, the currents of thought associated with such philosophers became universally accessible. It was largely through the lodges that "ordinary" colonists learned of that lofty premise called "the rights of man." It was through the lodges that they learned the concept of the perfectibility of society. And the New World seemed to offer a species of blank slate, a species of laboratory in which social experiment was possible and the principles enshrined by Freemasonry could be applied in practice.

O ne of the key questions about the American War for Independence is how and why Britain contrived to lose it. For the war was not so much "won" by the American colonists as "lost" by Britain. Britain alone, quite

Baigent and Leigh suggest the British commanders were not as ruthless as they might have been in attempting to suppress the American Revolution. Despite a direct order from King George III, Lord Jeffrey Amherst refused to take command of the British troops in America, though he was willing to fight against any European enemy. His capacity for ruthlessness was not in question—he had quelled Pontiac's Rebellion in Ohio by distributing smallpox-infected blankets to the Indians. But he was unwilling to fight against his former American allies. *Portrait of Jeffrey Amherst, 1st Baron Amherst by James Watson, after Sir Joshua Reynolds. © National Portrait Gallery, London.*

independently of the colonists' efforts, had the capacity to win or lose the conflict; and by not actively choosing to win it, she lost it more or less by default.

In most conflicts…victory or defeat by one or another combatant can be explained in military terms. In most such conflicts, the historian can point to one or more specific factors—certain tactical or strategic decisions, certain campaigns, certain battles, certain logistic considerations (such as supply lines or volume of industrial production), or simply the process of attrition. Any of these factors, the historian can say, either individually or in combination, brought about the collapse of one of the combatants, or rendered it untenable for one of the combatants to continue fighting. In the American War for Independence, however, there are no such factors to which the historian can satisfactorily point. Even the two battles usually regarded as "decisive"—Saratoga and Yorktown—can be regarded as "decisive" only in terms of American morale, or perhaps, with the wisdom of hindsight, in terms of intangible "watersheds." Neither of these engagements crippled, or even seriously impaired Britain's capacity to continue fighting. Neither involved more than a fraction of the British

troops deployed in North America. The war was to continue for four years after Saratoga, during which time the British defeat was redressed by a series of victories. And when Cornwallis surrendered at Yorktown, the bulk of the British forces in North America were still intact, still well-placed to continue operations elsewhere, still strategically and numerically in a position of advantage. There was, in the American War for Independence, no conclusive victory comparable to Waterloo, no ineluctable "turning point" comparable to Gettysburg. It seems almost as if everyone simply got tired, became bored, lost interest, decided to pack up and go home.

In American history textbooks, certain standard explanations are routinely presented as military explanations for the British defeat—because, of course, any such military explanation amounts to a testimonial of American prowess at arms. Thus, for example, it is often suggested, if not quite explicitly stated, that the whole of colonial North America was up in arms, confronting Britain with a hostile continent arrayed against her—a situation akin to that of Napoleon's or Hitler's invasion of Russia, with an entire people united to repel the aggressor. More often still, it is maintained that the

British Army was out of its element in the wilderness of North America—was untrained and unadapted to the kind of irregular guerrilla fighting employed by the colonists and dictated by the terrain. And it is often generally maintained that the British commanders were incompetent, inept, lazy, corrupt, out-thought and out-maneuvered. It is worth looking at each of these assertions individually.

In fact, the British Army was not confronted by a continent or a people passionately united against it. Of the thirty-seven newspapers in the colonies in 1775, twenty-three were in favor of the rebellion, seven were loyal to Britain and seven were neutral or uncommitted. If this can be taken to reflect the attitudes of the populace, fully 38 percent were not prepared to support independence. In reality, a substantial number of colonists remained actively attached to what they regarded as the mother country. They voluntarily spied, voluntarily furnished information, accommodation and supplies to British troops. Many of them actually resorted to arms and campaigned, alongside British regular units, against their colonial neighbors. In the course of the war, there were no fewer than fourteen regiments of "Loyalists" affiliated with the British Army.

> Opportunities were blandly ignored which would have been seized or pounced upon by far less efficient men.

Neither is it tenable to argue that the British Army was unsuited and untrained for the kind of warfare being waged in North America. In the first place, and contrary to popular impressions, most campaigning of the conflict did not involve irregular fighting at all. Most of it involved set-piece battles and sieges of precisely the kind being fought in Europe, precisely the kind at which the British Army, and the Hessian mercenaries within it, excelled. But even when irregular warfare was employed, British troops were at no disadvantage. As we have seen, Amherst, Wolfe and their subordinates, a mere twenty years before, had employed precisely that kind of warfare in wresting North America from France. In fact, the British Army had pioneered the sort of fighting sometimes dictated by the forests and rivers in which the techniques and formations of the European battlefield were out of place. Hessian troops might have been vulnerable to such tactics, but British units like 60th Foot—Ambrose's old rifle regiment—could outdo (and often outdid) the colonists at their own game, a game which, after all, most of the colonists' military leaders had learned from British commanders.

There remains the charge of incompetence and ineptitude on the part of the British commanders. So far as one of those commanders is concerned—Sir John Burgoyne—the charge is probably valid. As for the three primary commanders, however—Sir William Howe, Sir Henry Clinton and Lord Charles Cornwallis—it is not. In fact, Howe, Clinton and Cornwallis were quite as competent as their American counterparts. All three of them won more victories against the colonists than they lost—and larger, more substantial victories. All three of them had previously demonstrated their skill, and would have occasion to demonstrate it again. Howe, in particular, had played a prominent role in the war against the French twenty years before—had learned irregular tactics from his brother who died at Ticonderoga, had served under Amherst at Louisbourg and Montreal,

had led Wolfe's troops up the Heights of Abraham at Quebec. And between 1772 and 1774, he was responsible for the introduction of light infantry companies into line regiments. Clinton had been born in Newfoundland, had grown up in Newfoundland and New York, had served in the New York militia before joining the Guards and seeing action on the Continent, where his rise in the military hierarchy has been described as "meteoric." Cornwallis also distinguished himself during the Seven Years War. Subsequently, during the fighting in Mysore, he was to win a string of victories that gave Britain control of southern India—and, in the process, was to act as mentor to the young Sir Arthur Wellesley, later Duke of Wellington. And during the 1798 rebellion in Ireland, Cornwallis proved himself not just a skilled strategist, but also a wise and humane man, who had constantly to curb the over-zealous brutality of his subordinates. These were not, in short, inept or incompetent commanders.

But if the British high command during the American War for Independence was not incompetent or inept, it was—to a degree never satisfactorily explained by historians—strangely dilatory, desultory, apathetic, even torpid. Opportunities were blandly ignored which would have been seized or pounced upon by far less efficient men. Operations were conducted with an almost somnambulistic, lackadaisical air. The war, quite simply, was not pursued with the kind of ruthlessness required for victory—the kind of ruthlessness displayed by the same commanders when pitted against adversaries other than the American colonists.

In fact, Britain did not lose the war in North America for military reasons at all. The war was lost because of other, entirely different factors. It was a deeply unpopular war…with the British public, with most of the British government, with virtually all the British personnel directly involved—soldiers, officers and commanders. Clinton and Cornwallis both fought under duress, and with extreme reluctance. Howe was even more adamant, repeatedly expressing his anger, his unhappiness and his frustration about the command with which he had been saddled. His brother, Admiral Howe, felt the same way. The colonists, he declared, were "the most oppressed and distressed people on the earth."

Amherst's position was more militant still. At the outbreak of hostilities, Amherst was fifty-nine—fifteen years older than Washington, twelve years older than Howe, but still perfectly capable of conducting operations. Following his successes in the Seven Years War, he had become governor of Virginia, and had further developed his skills in irregular warfare during the Indian rebellion led by Chief Pontiac. When the American War for Independence began, he was commander-in-chief of the British Army, and had been chafing against the bureaucracy and tedium of his "desk job." Had Amherst taken command in North America, and (together with his old subordinate, Howe) campaigned with the vigor he had displayed against the French twenty years before, events would unquestionably have fallen out differently. But Amherst exhibited the same distaste as those who did grudgingly take the field; and his superior rank permitted him the luxury of refusal. The first offer came in 1776, and Amherst declined it. In January, 1778, he was approached again. This time he was not even asked. The king, George III, actually appointed him commander-in-chief in America and demanded that he take control of the war there. Threatening to resign his commission, Amherst refused the king's direct order. Attempts to persuade him by members of the government proved equally futile.

For Amherst, for Howe, for most of the other British commanders, as for the bulk of the British public at large, the American War for Independence was perceived as a kind of civil war. In effect, they found themselves, to their own discomfiture, pitted against adversaries whom they could only regard as fellow Englishmen—often linked to them not just by language, heritage, customs and attitudes, but also, in many cases, by actual family ties. But there was even more to it than that. As we have seen, Freemasonry, in eighteenth-century Britain, was a network pervading the whole of society, and particularly the educated classes—the professional people, the civil servants and administrators, the educators, the men who shaped and determined public opinion. It also engendered a general psychological and cultural climate, an atmosphere which suffused the mentality of the age. This was especially true in the military, where the field lodges constituted a cohesive structure binding men to their units, to their commanders and to one another. And it was even more true among "ordinary soldiers," who lacked the ties of caste and family which obtained in the officer class. During the American War for Independence, most of the military personnel involved, commanders and men on both sides, were either practicing Freemasons themselves, or were steeped in the attitudes and values of Freemasonry. The sheer prevalence of field lodges ensured that even non-Freemasons were constantly exposed to the institution's ideals. It could not fail to be apparent that many of those ideals were embodied by what the colonists were fighting for. The principles on behalf of which the colonists declared and then fought for independence were—incidentally, perhaps, but still pervasively—Freemasonic. And thus, for the British high command, as well as for the "rank-and-file," they were engaged in a war not just with fellow Englishmen, but also with Freemasonic brethren. In such circumstances, it was often difficult to be ruthless. This is not to suggest, of course, that British commanders were guilty of treason. They were, after all, professional soldiers, and were prepared, however reluctantly, to do their duty. But they were at pains to define their duty as narrowly as possible, and do nothing more.

The Great Seal of the United States

Conspiracy buffs point to the unfinished pyramid, all-seeing eye and call for a "New World Order" that are printed on our one-dollar bill as ample evidence of the Freemasonic conspiracy to rule the world. The roundel that contains these images is the reverse of the Great Seal of the United States, which has never been minted. In fact, it had never been published until Vice President Henry Wallace (a Freemason) convinced President Franklin Roosevelt (a Freemason) to incorporate it into the design of the new currency being issued in 1935.

Bill Moyers worked as a television news commentator and has had an extensive involvement with public television, producing documentaries and news journal programs. In 1988, Bill Moyers's PBS series *The Power of Myth* explored with Joseph Campbell the contents of his book on mythological, religious, and psychological archetypes. Joseph Campbell was an American mythologist, writer, and lecturer, best known for his work in comparative mythology and comparative religion.

Bill Moyers and Joseph Campbell explored the meaning of the Great Seal as part of their examination of The Power of Myth:

MOYERS: What kind of new myth do we need?

CAMPBELL: We need myths that will identify the individual not with his local group but with the planet. A model for that is the United States. Here were thirteen different little colony nations that decided to act in the mutual interest, without disregarding the individual interests of any one of them.

MOYERS: There is something about that on the Great Seal of the United States.

CAMPBELL: That's what the Great Seal is all about. I carry a copy of the Great Seal in my pocket in the form of a dollar bill. Here is the statement of the ideals that brought about the formation of the United States. Look at this dollar bill. Now here is the Great Seal of the United States. Look at the pyramid on the left. A pyramid has four sides. These are the four points of the compass. There

Freedom Plaza is a popular gathering spot in downtown Washington. In the pavement are the images from the Great Seal of the United States.

is somebody at this point, there's somebody at that point, and there's somebody at this point. When you're down on the lower levels of this pyramid, you will be either on one side or on the other. But when you get up to the top, the points all come together, and there the eye of God opens.

Robert Langdon and Katherine Solomon pretend the Seal secretly directs them to the George Washington Masonic Memorial in Alexandria, Virginia, in order to throw the CIA off their trail.

MOYERS: And to them it was the god of reason.

CAMPBELL: Yes. This is the first nation in the world that was ever established on the basis of reason instead of simply warfare. These were eighteenth-century deists, these gentlemen. Over here we read, "In God We Trust." But that is not the god of the Bible. These men did not believe in a Fall. They did not think the mind of man was cut off from God. The mind of man, cleansed of secondary and merely temporal concerns, beholds with the radiance of a cleansed mirror a reflection of the rational mind of God. Reason puts you in touch with God. Consequently, for these men, there is no special revelation anywhere, and none is needed, because the mind of man cleared of its fallibilities is sufficiently capable of the knowledge of God. All people in the world are thus capable because all people in the world are capable of reason.

All men are capable of reason. That is the fundamental principle of democracy. Because everybody's mind is capable of true knowledge, you don't have to have a special authority, or a special revelation telling you that this is the way things should be.

MOYERS: *And these symbols come from mythology?*
CAMPBELL: Yes, but they come from a certain quality of mythology. It's not the mythology of a special revelation. The Hindus, for example, don't believe in special revelation. They speak of a state in which the ears have opened to the song of the universe. Here the eyes have opened to the radiance of the mind of God. And that's a fundamental deist idea. Once you reject the idea of the Fall in the Garden, man is not cut off from his source.

Now back to the Great Seal. When you count the number of ranges on this pyramid, you find there are thirteen. And when you come to the bottom, there is an inscription in Roman numerals. It is, of course, 1776. Then, when you add one and seven and seven and six, you get twenty-one, which is the age of

reason, is it not? It was in 1776 that the thirteen states declared independence. The number thirteen is the number of transformation and rebirth. At the Last Supper there were twelve apostles and one Christ, who was going to die and be reborn. Thirteen is the number of getting out of the field of the bounds of twelve into the transcendent. You have twelve signs of the zodiac and the sun. These men were very conscious of the number thirteen as the number of resurrection and rebirth and new life, and they played it up here all the way through.

MOYERS: *But, as a practical matter, there were thirteen states.*
CAMPBELL: Yes, but wasn't that symbolic? This is not simply coincidental. This is the thirteen states as themselves symbolic of what they were.

MOYERS: *That would explain the other inscription down there, "Novus Ordo Seclorum."*
CAMPBELL: "A new order of the world." This is a new order of the world. And the saying above, *"Annuit Coeptis,"* means "He has smiled on our accomplishments" or "our activities."

MOYERS: *He—*

CAMPBELL: He, the eye, what is represented by the eye. Reason. In Latin you wouldn't have to say "he," it could be "it" or "she" or "he." But the divine power has smiled on our doings. And so this new world has been built in the sense of God's original creation, and the reflection of God's original creation, through reason, has brought this about.

If you look behind the pyramid, you see a desert. If you look before it, you see plants growing. The desert, the tumult of Europe, wars and wars and wars—we have pulled ourselves out of it and created a state in the name of reason, not in the name of power, and out of that will come the flowerings of the new life. That's the sense of that part of the pyramid.

Now look at the right side of the dollar bill. Here's the eagle, the bird of Zeus. The eagle is the down-coming of the god into the field of time. The bird is the incarnation principle of the deity. This is the bald eagle, the American eagle. This is the American counterpart of the eagle of the highest god, Zeus.

He comes down, descending into the world of the pairs of opposites, the field of action. One mode of action is war and the other is peace. So in one of his feet the eagle holds thirteen arrows—that's the principle of war. In the other he holds a laurel leaf with thirteen leaves—that is the principle of peaceful conversation. The eagle is looking in the direction of the laurel. That is the way these idealists who founded our country would wish us to be looking, to diplomatic relationships and so forth. But thank God he's got the arrows in the other foot, in case this doesn't work.

Now, what does the eagle represent? He represents what is indicated in this radiant sign above his head. I was lecturing once at the Foreign Service Institute in Washington on Hindu mythology, sociology, and politics. There's a saying in the Hindu book of politics that the ruler must hold in one hand the weapon of war, the big stick, and in the other the peaceful sound of the song of cooperative action. And there I was, standing with my two hands like this, and everybody in the room laughed. I couldn't understand. And then they began pointing. I looked back, and here was this picture of the eagle hanging on the wall behind my head in just the same posture that I was in. But when I looked, I also noticed this sign above his head, and that there were nine feathers in his tail. Nine is the number of the descent of the divine power into the world. When the Angelus rings, it rings nine times.

Now, over on the eagle's head are thirteen stars arranged in the form of a Star of David.

MOYERS: This used to be Solomon's Seal.
CAMPBELL: Yes. Do you know why it's called Solomon's Seal?

MOYERS: No.
CAMPBELL: Solomon used to seal monsters and giants and things into jars. You remember in the *Arabian Nights* when they'd open the jar and out would come the genie? I noticed the Solomon's Seal here, composed of thirteen stars and then I saw that each of the triangles were a Pythagorean tetrakys.

MOYERS: The tetrakys being?
CAMPBELL: This is a triangle composed of ten points, one point in the middle and four points to each side, adding up to nine: one, two, three, four/ five, six, seven/eight, nine. This is the primary symbol of Pythagorean philosophy, susceptible to a number of interrelated mythological, cosmological, psychological, and sociological interpretations, one of which is the dot at the apex as representing the creative center

out of which the universe and all things have come.

MOYERS: The center of energy, then?
CAMPBELL: Yes. The initial sound (a Christian might say, the creative Word), out of which the whole world was precipitated, the big bang, the pouring of the transcendent energy into and expanding through the field of time. As soon as it enters the field of time, it breaks into pairs of opposites, the one becomes two. Now, when you have two, there are just three ways in which they can relate to one another: one way is of this one dominant over that; another way is of that one dominant over this; and a third way is of the two in balanced accord. It is then, finally, out of these three manners of relationship that all things within the four quarters of space derive.

There is a verse in Lao-tzu's Tao-te Ching which states that out of the Tao, out of the transcendent, comes the One. Out of the One come Two; out of the Two come Three; and out of the Three come all things.

So what I suddenly realized when I recognized that in the Great Seal of the United States there were two of these symbolic triangles interlocked was that we now had thirteen points, for our thirteen original states, and that there were now, furthermore, no less than six apexes, one above, one below, and four (so to say) to the four quarters. The sense of this, it seemed to me, might be that from above or below, or from any point of the compass, the creative Word might be heard, which is the great thesis of democracy. Democracy assumes that anybody from any quarter can speak, and speak truth, because his mind is not cut off from the truth. All he has to do is clear out his passions and then speak.

So what you have here on the dollar bill is the eagle representing this wonderful image of the way in which the transcendent manifests itself in the world. That's what the United States is founded on. If you're going to govern properly, you've got to govern from the apex of the triangle, in the sense of the world eye at the top.

Now, when I was a boy, we were given George Washington's farewell address and told to outline the whole thing, every single statement in relation

John Trumbull's *Declaration of Independence* is one of four historical paintings by the artist placed in the Capitol Rotunda in the 1820s. Trumbull was a Revolutionary War officer and knew many of the signers, painting most of them from life.

to every other one. So I remember it absolutely. Washington said, "As a result of our revolution, we have disengaged ourselves from involvement in the chaos of Europe." His last word was that we not engage in foreign alliances. Well, we held on to his words until the First World War. And then we canceled the Declaration of Independence and rejoined the British conquest of the planet. And so we are now on one side of the pyramid. We've moved from one to two. We are politically, historically, now a member of one side of an argument. We do not represent that principle of the eye up there. And all of our concerns have to do with economics and politics and not with the voice and sound of reason.

MOYERS: *The voice of reason—is that the philosophical way suggested by these mythological symbols?*
CAMPBELL: That's right. Here you have the important transition that took place about 500 B.C. This is the date of the Buddha and of Pythagoras and Confucius and Lao-tzu, if there was a Lao-tzu. This is the awakening of man's reason. No longer is he informed and governed by the animal powers. No longer is he guided by the analogy of the planted earth, no longer by the courses of the planets—but by reason.

MOYERS: *The way of—*
CAMPBELL: —the way of man. And of course what destroys reason is passion. The principle passion in politics is greed. That is what pulls you down. And that's why we're on this side instead of the top of the pyramid.

MOYERS: *That's why our founders opposed religious intolerance—*
CAMPBELL: That was out entirely. And that's why they rejected the idea of the Fall, too. All men are competent to know the mind of God. There is no revelation special to any people.

MOYERS: *I can see how, from your years of scholarship and deep immersion in these mythological symbols, you would read the Great Seal that way. But wouldn't it have been surprising to most of those men who were deists, as you say, to discover these mythological connotations about their effort to build a new country?*
CAMPBELL: Well, why did they use them?

MOYERS: *Aren't a lot of these Masonic symbols?*

CAMPBELL: They are Masonic signs, and the meaning of the Pythagorean tetrakis has been known for centuries. The information would have been found in Thomas Jefferson's library. These were, after all, learned men. The eighteenth-century Enlightenment was a world of learned gentlemen. We haven't had men of that quality in politics very much. It's an enormous good fortune for our nation that that cluster of gentlemen had the power and were in a position to influence events at the time.

MOYERS: *What explains the relationship between these symbols and the Masons, and the fact that so many of these founding fathers belonged to the Masonic order? Is the Masonic order an expression somehow of mythological thinking?*

CAMPBELL: Yes, I think it is. This is a scholarly attempt to reconstruct an order of initiation that would result in spiritual revelation. These founding fathers who were Masons actually studied what they could of Egyptian lore. In Egypt, the pyramid represents the primordial hillock. After the annual flood of the Nile begins to sink down, the first hillock is symbolic of the reborn world. That's what this seal represents.

MOYERS: *You sometimes confound me with the seeming contradiction at the heart of your own belief system. On the one hand, you praise the men who were inspirers and creatures of the Age of Reason, and on the other hand, you salute Luke Skywalker in Star Wars for that moment when he says, "Turn off the computer and trust your feelings." How do you reconcile the role of science, which is reason, with the role of faith, which is religion?*

CAMPBELL: No, no, you have to distinguish between reason and thinking.

MOYERS: *Distinguish between reason and thinking? If I think, am I not reasoning things out?*

CAMPBELL: Yes, your reason is one kind of thinking. But thinking things out isn't necessarily reason in this sense. Figuring out how you can break through a wall is not reason. The mouse who figures out, after it bumps its nose here, that perhaps he can get around there, is figuring something out the way we figure things out. But that's not reason. Reason has to do with finding the ground of being and the fundamental structuring of order of the universe.

MOYERS: So when these men talked about the eye of God being reason, they were saying that the ground of our being as a society, as a culture, as a people, derives from the fundamental character of the universe?

CAMPBELL: That's what this first pyramid says. This is the pyramid of the world, and this is the pyramid of our society, and they are of the same order. This is God's creation, and this is our society.

BROTHER DOUGHTY

I violate no secret when I say that one of the greatest values in Masonry is that it affords an opportunity for men in all walks of life to meet and have one common interest. For example, when I was President the Master of my lodge was Brother Doughty, gardener on the estate of one of my neighbors, and a most public spirited citizen with whom I liked to come in contact. Clearly I could not call upon him when I came home—it would have embarrassed him—neither could he, without embarrassment, call on me. In the lodge it was different. He was over me though I was President, and it was good for him and for me.

—THEODORE ROOSEVELT (RECOUNTED BY RAY V. DENSLOW IN *FREEMASONRY AND THE PRESIDENCY*)

Theodore Roosevelt as a Master Mason, 1912. J. L. Phelps. *Photo by David Bohl. Scottish Rite Museum and Library.*

FINDING THE LOST SYMBOLS IN WASHINGTON, D.C.

As they raced through the corridors of the Library of Congress, Langdon and Walter Bellamy (Architect of the Capitol) might have caught a glimpse of the Capitol, a quarter of a mile away. *Library of Congress, Prints & Photographs Division. Photograph by Carol M. Highsmith.*

The Library of Congress

With the Architect of the Capitol, Robert Langdon escapes from the Capitol Visitor Center through a tunnel to the Library of Congress. Still under construction during their flight, the tunnel is now complete.

The Library of Congress provides a warm welcome to readers and tourists as they emerge from the tunnel. The crowds in the Visitor Center and the Rotunda, and the understandably tense police force obliged to protect Congress and the Capitol, are quickly forgotten. Library visitors are encouraged to take their time, look up at the marvelous architecture, sculpture, and painting, and contemplate the soaring potential of human knowledge.

Unlike in Philadelphia and New York, where college libraries and private collections had been available to members of Congress, Washington, in 1800, hardly contained any books. The newly arrived Congress appropriated $5,000, and 740 books and 30 maps were purchased from London. The collection was narrow, comprised mostly of law books, and had only 3,000 volumes when it was burned by the British in the War of 1812.

The tunnel that leads from the Capitol Visitor Center to the Library of Congress.

Former President Thomas Jefferson, then seventy-one years old, offered to sell his personal library to Congress. Fifty years in the making, it reflected the broad range of his own interests in philosophy, science, architecture, and literature, and he wished to sell it all, in the hope of paying off his debts. Perhaps to disarm opposition to the scope of the proposed acquisition, Jefferson wrote: "I do not know that it contains any branch of science which Congress would wish to exclude from their collection; there is, in fact, no subject to which a Member of Congress may not have occasion to refer."

Congress agreed to purchase all his 6,487 books for about $24,000. (Evidently, his library contained no books on global warming.)

In 1870, the Librarian of Congress Ainsworth Rand Spofford suggested his office become the Registrar of Copyrights, and that authors give two copies of each copyrighted work to the Library. Soon the shelves were inundated with books, prints, photographs, and other works. New construction was

Bellamy leads Langdon past two of the Library's most prized possessions, the hand-copied Bible of Mainz and an original printed Gutenberg Bible, both from the 1450s. On the ceiling above are the murals of *The Evolution of the Book,* by John White Alexander (pictured below, and bottom right).

Library of Congress, Prints & Photographs Division. Photograph by Carol M. Highsmith.

authorized, and what is now known as the Thomas Jefferson Building, where Langdon and Bellamy take refuge, was completed in 1897. Its magnificence is the result of the efforts of numerous architects and engineers and two Senators who dedicated themselves to the Library's funding and administration. The contributions of over fifty artists fill the interior of the building.

The Library of Congress now contains nearly 150 million items. A project to digitize significant portions of its collection and make it available on the Internet is ongoing.

As Bellamy and Langdon examine the pyramid, from high above the *Evolution of Civilizations* overlooks them. *Photo: Library of Congress, Prints & Photographs Division. Photograph by Carol M. Highsmith.*

Bellamy and Langdon enter the Main Reading Room, a spectacular space but one that hardly appears to offer much refuge. *Photo: Library of Congress, Prints & Photographs Division. Photograph by Carol M. Highsmith.*

A statue of Moses is among a series of sixteen peering out from the balustrade of the Reading Room. The horns on the figure, long a traditional element in renderings of Moses, occasion a discussion between Langdon and Bellamy about how a single mistake, in this case a Latin mistranslation from Hebrew, can reverberate throughout history. *Photo: Library of Congress, Prints & Photographs Division. Photograph by Carol M. Highsmith.*

92

With Katherine Solomon frantically trying to gain entry at the front door, Bellamy and Langdon cross the Great Hall to let her in. *Photo: Library of Congress, Prints & Photographs Division. Photograph by Carol M. Highsmith.*

The library is normally closed at night, but the characters of the *The Lost Symbol*
find it a very hospitable place as they attempt to decipher the ancient mysteries.
Library of Congress, Prints & Photographs Division. Photograph by Carol M. Highsmith.

CHAPTER THREE
Pierre L'Enfant and the Founding of Washington, D.C.

**The Constitution of the United States,
Article 1. Section 8.**

*The Congress shall have Power to exercise exclusive
Legislation in all Cases whatsoever, over such District
(not exceeding ten Miles square) as may, by Cession of
particular States, and the Acceptance of Congress,
become the Seat of the Government of the United States....*

The Great Dinner   *By Michael Bober*

Michael Bober is a filmmaker who has produced two documentaries concerning the American Revolution, Favorite Son: Alexander Hamilton *and* The Making of Mary Silliman's War.

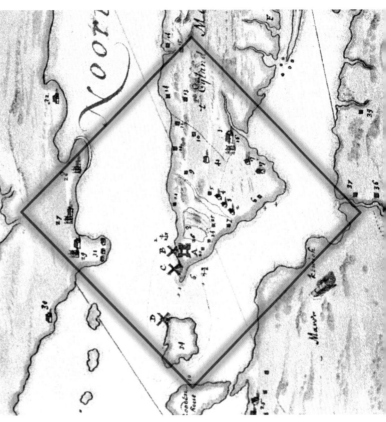

A ten-mile-square "federal district," with lower Manhattan in the center, superimposed upon an early Dutch map. *Michael Bober and Laura Smyth.*

The framers of the Constitution were well aware Congress and the other branches of the federal government needed a permanent home. Since the convening of the First Continental Congress in 1774, the lawmakers had often found themselves on the run, not just from British troops but from angry American veterans demanding payment for their service during the Revolution. Perhaps this history of fear and exile inspired Article 1, Section 8, of the Constitution which granted vast power to Congress over the federal district that would include the capital city.

The first United States Congress met in 1789 in New York, and it is not inconceivable it could have remained there. The ten-mile-square district proposed by the Constitution could easily

At left, L'Enfant's 1791 plan.

have encompassed much of Manhattan and portions of Brooklyn and New Jersey, with control over the rivers and port of New York. It is tempting to imagine the state of American politics in the twenty-first century if New Yorkers, Brooklynites, and New Jerseyans were subject to the "Power" of Congress "in all Cases whatsoever," and denied the right to vote.

But that fate came to be reserved for the people of Washington, D.C., largely as the result of a deal between President Washington's Treasury Secretary, Alexander Hamilton, and his Secretary of State, Thomas Jefferson.

Hamilton and Jefferson, about to embark upon a decade of opposition in every matter of policy and philosophy to be considered in the early Republic, had never met when Jefferson arrived in New York, the first capital city, in March 1790.

Hamilton was already embroiled with Congress over a very divisive issue—whether the states would remain individually responsible for the debts they incurred during the Revolutionary War, or whether, as he proposed, the new federal government would assume them. To Hamilton, the cohesiveness, economic potential, and very survival of

the United States depended on the federal assumption of the states' debts.

Congress found itself deadlocked over another question as well, and the sentiments surrounding it are well described by Henry Cabot Lodge, a turn-of-the-century Senator and historian:

> This matter of the seat of government had excited great controversy and feeling between States and sections. Whether the future capital should be in New York or Pennsylvania, in Virginia or Maryland; whether this inestimable boon should fall to the North or to the South, was a burning question second only to assumption. Local prejudice and local pride were raised to white heat on this momentous issue.

> To Hamilton all this was supremely indifferent…

> While he was purely and intensely national in opinion, and was devotedly attached to the United States, he was utterly devoid of local feeling and state pride. There is no evidence that he cared one whit, except as a matter of abstract

convenience, where Congress fixed the site of the federal city.

Secretary Jefferson soon became acquainted with his fellow cabinet member. In his autobiography he recalls an early meeting:

Thomas Jefferson by Charles Wilson Peale. *Independence National Historical Park.*

Hamilton was in despair.... He painted pathetically the temper into which the legislature had been wrought, the disgust of those who were called the Creditor states, the danger of the secession of their members, and the separation of the states. He observed that the members of the administration ought to act in concert, and...it was probable that an appeal from me to the judgment and discretion of some of my friends might effect a change....

I told him that if a dissolution of our union at this incipient stage were endangered, I should deem that the most unfortunate of all consequences....I proposed to him however to dine with me the next day, and I would invite another friend or two...and I thought it impossible that reasonable men, consulting together cooly, could fail, by some mutual sacrifices of opinion, to form a compromise which was to save the union.

There had been propositions to fix the seat of government either at Philadelphia, or at Georgetown on the Potomac; and it was thought by giving it to Philadelphia for ten years, and to Georgetown permanently afterwards, this might, as an anodyne, calm in some degree the ferment.

Jefferson eventually came to think Hamilton got the better part of the deal.

ON APRIL 15, 1791,

the southernmost boundary stone—"home plate" of the diamond of the District of Columbia—was ceremoniously laid at Jones Point in Alexandria, Virginia. An African American astronomer, Benjamin Banneker, made the celestial observations necessary to ascertain the exact location. Subsequent stones were placed at one-mile intervals around the periphery of the District.

The boundary markers fared badly during the nineteenth century, as many were defaced or stolen. In 1915, the Washington, D.C., chapter of the Daughters of the American Revolution assumed responsibility for protecting them.

The history and exact locations of the stones can be found at www.boundarystones.org.

This Civil War–era map (1862) shows the original borders of the federal district, despite the fact that the west side of the Potomac had been ceded back to Virginia in 1846. It also reveals the fortifications defending Washington from the Confederacy—which is why the War Department withdrew it two days after mistakenly putting it on sale.

Right: "Home plate" boundary stone at Jones Point Lighthouse, Alexandria, Virginia. Far Right: Looking south over the boundary stone down the Potomac toward George Washington's Mount Vernon.

Indeed, as Lodge makes clear, he wasn't really giving anything up.

Hamilton was no doubt aware of the desire of President Washington to situate the capital on the Potomac, near his beloved Mount Vernon. It would have been impolitic indeed for the Treasury Secretary not to defer to his Chief on this sensitive matter. Washington saw the Potomac as the future highway to the West—the Ohio Valley—believing it would become a great river of commerce. It is even possible that Hamilton may have favored such a remote capital, where the federal government might stretch wide its powers, relatively undisturbed by entrenched local interests.

Whatever the motives, Congressman James Madison, the other special guest with Hamilton at Jefferson's table that evening, dropped his opposition to the Assumption, and with Jefferson's support brought the Virginia delegation into line. Hamilton, meanwhile, persuaded New York representatives to support the Southern location for the capital.

On July 1, 1790, the Senate voted by a margin of 14 to 12 to locate the permanent capital city on the Maryland side of the Potomac River. On July 9, the House concurred by a vote of 32 to 29, and on July 16 President Washington signed The Residence Act into law.

It could be said that even today Alexander Hamilton presides over the Treasury Department. On the base of the statue are the words of Daniel Webster about Hamilton: "He smote the rock of the national resources and abundant streams of revenue gushed forth. He touched the dead corpse of the public credit and it sprang upon its feet."

Pierre L'Enfant Designs the Federal City

President Washington personally guided the new capital's development. He considered various sites along the Potomac and decided upon a stretch between the port of Georgetown, Maryland, and the mouth of the Anacostia River. Alexandria, Virginia, where the President owned land, was also included within the diamond-shaped boundary of the Federal District, but there was to be no government sponsored construction there. Washington was determined to dispel any hint of personal interest as he presided over the creation of the Federal City.

George Town and Federal City, or City of Washington by T. Cartwright, 1801.

The President appointed a Board of Commissioners and asked Major Andrew Ellicott to make a survey and map. He then chose Pierre L'Enfant to design the city's plan and to serve as the chief architect. Born in France, his father a painter in the Court of Louis XV, L'Enfant had served with Lafayette during the Revolutionary War, eventually joining General Washington's staff. As an engineer and architect, L'Enfant was behind almost every contemporary project of note, including the conversion of New York's City Hall into Federal Hall, the site of Washingon's inauguration and the seat of the First Congress.

L'Enfant's vision stretched far into the future:

This image of Pierre L'Enfant, created by Sarah De Hart in 1785, is the only one known that was done from life. *United States Department of State.*

> No nation, perhaps, had ever before the opportunity offered them of deliberately deciding on the spot where their Capital City should be fixed.... The plans should be drawn on such a scale as to leave room for that aggrandizement and embellishment which the increase of the wealth of the nation will permit it to pursue at any period, however remote.

L'Enfant chose the sites for the Capitol and the President's House, and envisioned a great boulevard to connect them:

> Every grand building would rear with a majestied aspect over the Country all around and might be advantageously seen from twenty miles off.... The Federal City would soon grow of itself and spread as the branches of a tree do.

In August 1791, L'Enfant presented his completed plan to Washington and Jefferson. Grand radial avenues "to and from principal places"—superimposed upon a more conventional rectangular

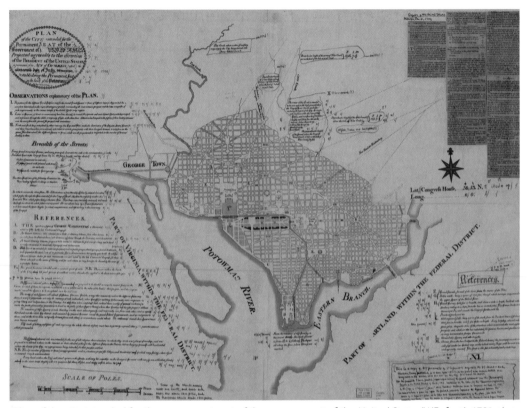

"Plan of the city intended for the permanent seat of the government of the United States." L'Enfant's 1791 plan, along with Jefferson's handwritten notes, are included in this facsimile created by the U.S. Coast and Geodetic Survey in 1887.

grid—provide a "reciprocity of sight," and "a rapid intercourse with all parts of the city, to which they will serve as does the main artery in the animal body." Public squares, monuments, and fountains would occupy the intersections of the avenues and surround government buildings.

Both the President and his Secretary of State were overwhelmed with its magnificence.

Meanwhile, Washington's appointed Commissioners settled upon a plan where federal properties would be auctioned to private owners to provide funds for the construction of the city.

L'Enfant immediately perceived this proposed "checkerboard" pattern of public and private lots as fatal to his plan. It would provide fertile ground for countless neighbors' quarrels, all impeding the progress of great public works. He perceived the interests of the Commissioners to be merely pecuniary, while his vision contemplated the historic dimensions of the new Republic—the unique grandeur appropriate to the Capital of the United States.

L'Enfant refused to provide his map for the first sale of lots. Then he engaged in a dispute with a nephew of one of the Commissioners,

This copy of Edward Savage's *The Washington Family* shows Martha Washington pointing to a map of the Capital City, as it was often called in the 1790s. *DeWint House, Tappan, NY.*

who had begun to construct a house that L'Enfant deemed would cross the future diagonal route of New Jersey Avenue. Threats ensued, and L'Enfant told the Commissioners:

> Respecting the house of Mr. Carroll…I directed yesterday forenoon a number of hands to the spot….The roof is already down with part of the brickwork and the whole will I expect be leveled to the ground before the week is over."

The Commissioners informed Washington that L'Enfant had demolished Mr. Carroll's house, though still

"expressing a hope that the affair may be still so adjusted that we may not Lose his services."

Washington, well aware of L'Enfant's temperament, urged the Commissioners to accommodate him:

> His pride would be gratified, and his ambition excited by such a mark of your confidence. If…he should take amiss and leave the business, I have no scruple in declaring to you (although I do not want him to know it) that I know not where another is to be found, who could supply his place.

To L'Enfant himself, the President issued a warning:

> I can only once more, and now for all, inform you that every matter and thing which has relation to the Federal district, and the City within it, is committed to the Commissioners appointed.

Unwilling to submit, L'Enfant renounced "the pursuit of that fame which the success of the undertaking must procure, rather than to engage to conduct it under a system which would not only... crush its growth but make me appear the principal cause of the destruction of it."

Informed that his services were at an end, L'Enfant declined a $2,500 offer, petitioning for much higher compensation. After eight years he finally accepted it, telling President Jefferson in 1801 that "the only reproach to which I may be liable...is my having been more faithfull to a principle than ambition." L'Enfant died in 1825 in poverty and obscurity.

Deprived of L'Enfant's services as architect, Secretary of State Jefferson invited submissions for the designs of the Capitol and the President's house. For three months, no plans appeared. When a design for the Capitol was finally accepted, problems with its execution ensued. On the day Washington laid the Capitol cornerstone—September 17, 1793—its future form was still unknown. The Capitol was not to be completed for 71 years.

The Mall, seen from the west stairway of the Capitol, which presidents now use to enter the portico for their inaugurations. The Mall can accommodate crowds of well over one million people.

Similarly the house President Jefferson moved into after his election in 1800 was far from complete. Sustaining great damage from British mayhem in the War of 1812, the White House was not completed until 1833.

And it was not until 1901 that L'Enfant's plan reemerged. A new federal commission finally put many of its ideas into effect. The Mall was expanded and truly became what L'Enfant intended, "a place of general resort," the public space for the nation. The deference offered by the renowned architects on the commission—Daniel Burnham, Charles McKim, and Frederick Law Olmstead, Jr.—to L'Enfant's great original vision restored his name to history. In 1909, his remains were transferred to a tomb atop Arlington National Cemetery, overlooking the Capital City whose form he had dreamt into being.

L'Enfant's tomb at Arlington National Cemetery.

Pierre L'Enfant and the Sacred Geometry of Washington, D.C. *by Nicholas R. Mann*

Nicholas R. Mann is the author the Sacred Geometry of Washington, D.C.

In his design for the capital city of the New World, the eighteenth-century architect Major Pierre Charles L'Enfant followed the pattern of the architectural re- "Creation of the world" by first establishing a new world center, an axis mundi, in the site for the U.S. Capitol, the House of Congress. L'Enfant conceived of the Capitol as a primary point of origin in the center of the new country, with one vertical and two horizontal axes passing through it. He established an east-west axis across Washington with the Mall and East Capitol Street, and a north-south axis, that was to function additionally as a new, global, zero-degree meridian, running through North and South Capitol Streets. As is well known in Freemasonry, this creation of the symbolic definition of the world center and the six directions is the first step in all traditional sacred geometry. Marking the center and the cardinal directions were the first acts in the highly ritualized and geometrical laying out of any

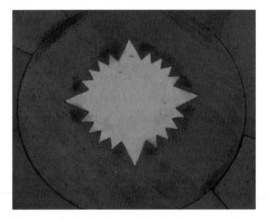

The compass in the floor of the Capitol crypt beneath the Rotunda marks the zero meridian for the layout of the city, and symbolically for the entire nation. The crypt was intended to contain the tomb of George Washington, but his remains were never transferred from Mount Vernon.

temple in classical, Egyptian, Hindu or any other architectural tradition.

The subsequent steps taken by L'Enfant demonstrate that he used the unique proportion of the Golden Section to determine the placement of the city's avenues, the squares, the White House, the Supreme Court, the monuments, the memorials, the streets, the commercial districts, City Hall and the District Courts. Through an elaborate exercise in the pentagonal nature of traditional Golden Section geometry, the French architect created a "template"—a

Novus Ordo Seclorum or "new order of the ages"—for the Capital City of the new American Republic. His imagination fired by the unique opportunity to establish a center and an ideal foundational order for a country the like of which had never been seen before, the evidence clearly shows that L'Enfant followed the practice of ancient architectural tradition....

From his ideas and writings, such as his reports to President Washington, it is evident that although L'Enfant was an idealist and a gentleman, he was also a soldier, an engineer and a man of action. He was also an individualist and an iconoclast in that he rejected the imperialist and religious values of old Europe. Nowhere in any of his writings does L'Enfant say he applied predetermined geometrical principles, or any religious, Masonic or neoclassical ideas, or that he ever favored any existing city plan, or any specific metaphysical point of view. On the contrary, the evidence suggests he took pains to reject such patterns; declaring for example that he did not need Jefferson's plans of European cities. He always insisted upon the originality of his views. Despite his innate aristocratic tendencies (tendencies that were ultimately to be his downfall), L'Enfant

wanted no part of the religious, monarchic, imperialist and Old World values that his new nation had so recently liberated itself from. His sympathies entirely lay with American ideals of the new democratic Republic and also with the newly emerging sense of their national destiny being linked with the natural power of the vast landscape. He sought to express those ideals in a design for a new visionary city. When he found the basis for this design in the naturally occurring ratios of the Golden Section, true to his inflexible character, he would not tolerate any departure from the order that made the design a whole....

L'Enfant...found the inspiration for his architectural forms in nature. L'Enfant observed, surveyed, drew and lived with the landscape during his many years in the Revolutionary Army and he quickly took to the location that was to become the City of Washington. As many writers have remarked, in the 1790s L'Enfant was at the height of his physical powers—nature, perception, imagination, intuition, mind and body worked as one. He had fought in the war, received a wound, been imprisoned by the British, dined with the generals and been befriended by the powerful. By now his personal beliefs wholly conformed to his experience of the forming of the new American nation. He imposed no grid or preconceived mental order on the landscape, and abandoned aesthetic conventions that narrowed artistic expression into the service of a monarchy, or class-conscious ideas such as the "picturesque." In his search for "the real grand and truly beautiful" it seems that L'Enfant found in the landscape of Goose Creek and Jenkins Hill evocative, even sublime forms that were to shape a great, powerful and prosperous destiny for America....

Evidence may never be found that can confirm the specific sources of L'Enfant's inspiration. A traditional geometric order clearly informs his design for the city; but the way in which it was used indicates an original and open approach—the hallmark of a true artist. L'Enfant worked sensitively with the topography of the landscape, the consciousness of the American people, and his own creative genius. As the architect crossed and recrossed the landscape of the future city, its diverse forms inspired a new and compelling synthesis of politics and place.

Although slightly off the east-west axis envisioned by L'Enfant, the Mall on the equinox features a sunrise over the Capitol and a sunset into the Washington Monument.

FINDING THE LOST SYMBOLS IN WASHINGTON, D.C.

The Secrets of the Pods *by Loren Coleman*

Loren Coleman is a cryptozoologist, one who studies "hidden animals." He is the author of many books, including Cryptozoology A to Z, *and the director of the International Cryptozoology Museum in Portland, Maine.*

Dan Brown has turned a location that's right out of science fiction and creatures from ancient mythologies into a major set piece and characters in his new book.

The location is the Smithsonian Institution's Museum Support Center (MSC), a real site, located in Suitland, Maryland. Covering 4.5 acres and constructed in five "pods" (or buildings), the MSC has more than 500,000 square feet of space, in 12 miles of cabinets, with more than 31 million objects. It has routinely been compared to the last scene in the first Indiana Jones film, *Raiders of the Lost Ark*, where the vast warehouse is shown housing all the secrets discovered but unrevealed.

Opposite: The Alecton attempts to capture a giant squid off Tenerife in 1861. *Illustration from Harper Lee's Sea Monsters Unmasked, London, 1884*

Brown employs the strange structural uniqueness of the MSC for some of his most dramatic scenes. The MSC is laid out in a series of gigantic zigs and zags, with a wide corridor called the "Street" down its center like a spine, with offices and labs on one side, and the enormous storage pods opposite them. Each pod is huge, three stories high and the size of a football field. They all have high levels of security, temperature controls (constantly at 70 degrees), and humidity maintained at 50 percent. And as in the novel, each pod is set inside insulated walls a foot and a half thick, contained within a "dead zone" that is two feet wide to prevent any pests from invading the spaces.

The Museum Support Center was dedicated in May 1983, and Pod 5 was added in 2005, at a cost of 33 million dollars. (Hmm, interesting it should be $33,000,000 with all the Masonic symbolism of the number 33 in *The Lost Symbol*.)

While the notion of a secret lab studying "noetic sciences" in Pod 5 at the MSC is total fiction, the real pods do hold many incredibly wonderful

Smithsonian Museum Support Center.
Copyright © Smithsonian Museum.

treasures. In the novel, and until recently in real life, Pod 3, the so-called wet pod, is where you would have found the giant squid that the Smithsonian has in storage. The government's FY2009 budget reveals that the museum's collection of "vertebrate, invertebrate, and botanical collections stored in alcohol and other fluids" were moved from Pod 3 to Pod 5 in 2009.

In the "wet" pod are millions of specimens in glass jars, bottles, tanks and tubs, all of them preserved in 75 percent ethanol, the smell of which provides a clue in saving Katherine Solomon's life in the book. Kept in the wet pod are giant squids, known during ancient times as the legendary Kraken. Unrecognized by science until 1877, very few have ever been found dead and washed ashore on American shores.

The giant squid described in Brown's book matches the well-preserved specimen from Massachusetts. Found on a Plum Island beach in early 1980, it has a total length of nine feet. The Plum Island squid is now in Smithsonian scientist Clyde Roper's giant squid collection, which totals four.

Brown not only features a giant squid, an *Architeuthis*, a once "legendary" animal, in his novel but another ancient fish, one thought extinct for 65 million years until it was rediscovered in 1938. This fish, now in the new wet pod, is the famous coelacanth.

What are these newly discovered ancient fish doing in a novel about Freemasons, Washington, D.C., and noetic sciences? Actually, it's just more of Dan Brown doing what he so much likes to do—reveal ancient truths.

This Coelacanth, which was caught in 1974 off the Comoros Islands, is only one of 200 specimens captured since the species was rediscovered in 1938. *Photo by Alberto Fernandez Fernandez.*

CHAPTER FOUR
Noetic Science

The topic of consciousness is as vast as the cosmos and as close to us as sleep.

Star V838 Mon. *Photo courtesy NASA and the Hubble Heritage Team.*

A cape of electrodes is placed on a volunteer to monitor his brain wave activity during a distant intention experiment. *Photo by Kelly Durkin.*

Noetic Science   *by Edgar D. Mitchell*

Astronaut Edgar D. Mitchell established the Institute of Noetic Sciences shortly after he returned from the moon. This excerpt is drawn from his Introduction and Conclusion to Psychic Exploration: A Challenge to Science *(edited by John White).*

In February 1971, I had the privilege of walking on the moon as a member of the Apollo 14 lunar expedition. During the voyage I made a test in extrasensory perception (ESP), attempting to send information telepathically to four receivers on earth.

Since then, people have asked me why an astronaut would take such an intense interest in a subject as ridiculed and unacceptable in respectable scientific circles as psychic research.

It is a fair question. My real interest is—and has been for many years—to understand the nature of consciousness and the relationship of body to mind. Psychic research is one facet of this larger whole. Therefore, it might be said that I have simply gone from outer space to inner space.

The study of mind and consciousness is called noetics. The term comes from the Greek root word *nous*, meaning "mind." As popularly used, noetic refers to purely intellectual apprehension.

But Plato spoke of noetic knowledge as the highest form of knowing—a direct cognition or apprehension of the eternal truths that surpasses the normal discursive processes of logical, intellectual reasoning. The word *science*, of course, originally meant "knowing" but has come to mean a type of knowing derived from use of the objective, rational faculties of mind. But psychic abilities such as telepathy are another type of knowing—a subjective knowing, a nonrational, cognitive process largely overlooked by the scientific world. Consciousness appears to be the central, unifying concept behind these different aspects of mind. Thus, in the spirit of its Grecian origin, I propose to use the omega (Ω) as a symbol for consciousness and noetics.

The topic of consciousness is as vast as the cosmos and as close to us as sleep.

Noetics is the discipline that is arising from this confluence of outer- and inner-space research. It is the ultimate frontier in man's attempt to understand himself and the nature of the universe.

If we review the history of mankind's attempt to perceive, cognize, and interpret his environment, we find that in the last four centuries, as a result of the growth of scientific methodology, a formalized dichotomy has arisen between proponents of the two modes of knowing: objective observation (followed by deductive reasoning) and direct cognitive processes. These opposing modes of perception are crudely epitomized as science versus religion, reason versus intuition, rationality versus nonrationality, objective knowledge versus subjective experience, and so forth. Only in relatively recent years have scholars of each persuasion actively and vehemently denied the validity of the other process. In prescientific times, scholars whether they agreed upon their conclusions or not at least recognized the validity of both external and internal observation. (We must quickly add that the truly great teachers of modern times have always acknowledged this dual process.)

Thus, although I am identifying consciousness as the ultimate frontier in man's attempt to gain knowledge, it is by no means a new frontier because throughout history people have sought to resolve the differences between their objective methods and their subjective experience—between outer and inner. The study of mind and consciousness is the common ground for this effort. The living system that we call man is a holistic phenomenon that exhibits both modes of knowing.

Perhaps after 350 years of divisiveness between science and religion we are on the threshold of a new era of knowledge and cooperation. It should be obvious that objective observation and reason do not by themselves produce a satisfactory ethic for living—neither for the individual nor for social systems. Facts become divorced from values, and action from need.

On the other hand, intuition and inspiration do not, by themselves, produce the agreement society needs to bring about order, structure, and survival in the material world. In this case, observation frequently becomes subject to individual interpretation according to the covert biases of the individual.

The antagonism between the objective and subjective modes of knowledge can be clearly illustrated. In 1600 Giordano Bruno was burned at the stake by theologians for asserting that the earth was not the center of the solar system and that there were other solar systems with living beings in them. In 1972 the American Academy of Science asserted that science and religion are "mutually exclusive realms of thought" and therefore the Genesis theory of creation should be kept out of science textbooks. The roles of science and religion are reversed in the modern example, but the same closed-minded dogmatism is operating to limit inquiry through sanctimonious denial of other viewpoints.

> The proper direction of sophisticated instrumentation and laboratory techniques can be the means whereby the physical and metaphysical realms are shown to be different aspects of the same reality.

Research over the last fifty years by little-known, but forward-looking thinkers has shown there is a vast creative potential in the human mind that is as yet almost totally unrecognized by science. Nonrational cognitive processes have so far eluded scientific description. However, this potential has been previously known and described by a few ancient sages and enlightened religious teachers, using veiled prescientific language to express what they discovered through subjective, intuitive, experiential means. We are, in my opinion, on the threshold of rediscovering and redefining those concepts and insights through the objective, rational, experimental efforts of science—if dogmatism and outmoded belief structures do not prevent it. The proper direction of sophisticated instrumentation and laboratory techniques can be the means whereby the physical and metaphysical realms are shown to be different aspects of the same reality. If this is demonstrated, it would be ironic, but appropriate, that so-called godless technology and materialistic science should lead to the rediscovery of the essential unity of science and religion.

Noetics recognizes all this. Noetics is the research frontier where the convergence of objectivity and subjectivity, of reason and intuition, is occurring most rapidly. In the study of consciousness, the techniques and technology of science are being combined with the higher insights of mind from both East and West to provide a new methodology for scholarly inquiry. For it is quite clear that reason alone is not sufficient for total understanding of ourselves. As Michael Polanyi, the eminent philosopher of science, points out, scientific discoveries do not always follow in a sequence of perfectly logical deductions. Instead, many discoveries involve intuitions and hunches on the part of the scientist in a manner that cannot be completely explained.

Principles being discovered in noetic research demonstrate the underlying unity of science and religion. It is the key to transforming human consciousness from narrow egotism to cosmic altruism, thereby providing the basis for solutions to the world's major problems. From the noetic point of view, man's existence takes on significance and psychic research becomes a significant tool in the quest for self-understanding. The search for meaning involves regaining the self-knowledge that enlightened beings before us have had. "Who am I?" the saints and sages have asked throughout history. What is the nature of self, that it can be aware of being aware?

The question "Who am I?" may be restated as "What is consciousness?" Consciousness appears to be the essence of man and the universe. Man's purpose is to become more conscious, more aware of the nature of consciousness. Kathryn Breese-Whiting notes: "The ancients have stated that God sleeps in the mineral, awakens in the vegetable, walks in the animal and thinks in man." This beautifully summarizes my view. By expanding personal consciousness into transpersonal consciousness, we become a party by agreement to the functioning of the universe. Its existence becomes precious to us because it is us. The Bible says that in the beginning, God created the heavens and the earth. Since viewing earth from space, I have reconfirmed through personal experience what the ancient scriptures say. In a spirit of integration and harmony, then, between our rational, objective, experimental aspect and our intuitive, subjective, experiential aspect, perhaps we can restate that profound insight in modern idiom as the mark of a new age:

"In the beginning, Consciousness intended matter..."

Right: Ed Mitchell on the moon, February 1971. *Photo by SSPL/Getty Images.*

Toward Homo Noeticus   by John White

Excerpted from the introduction of Enlightenment 101 *by permission of the author.*

In 1972, I joined with Apollo 14 astronaut Edgar Mitchell to study the human mind and apply our findings to planetary problems. The research organization he founded the following year was called the Institute of Noetic Sciences (IONS). Noetics means the study of consciousness. I suggested that word for the institute's name at one of our planning sessions. I had adopted use of it from Dr. Charles Musés, editor of *Journal for the Study of Consciousness* (funded by Arthur M. Young, author of *The Reflexive Universe*), who in turn adopted it from Plato and William James, where its root form, *nous*, means "higher mind" or "ultimate mind." Musés (1919–2000) had been using the word since 1967 to denote scientific investigation of a wide range of phenomena and issues involving human awareness. In his 1972 book *Consciousness and Reality*, Musés defined noetics as "the science of the study of consciousness and its alterations."

In 1978, the late Dr. Willis Harman, then president of IONS, elaborated: "the noetic sciences are … the esoteric core of all the world's religions, East and West, ancient and modern, becoming exoteric"—i.e. "going public." He added, "A noetic science—a science of consciousness and the world of inner experience—is the most promising contemporary framework within which to carry on that fundamental moral inquiry which stable human societies have always had to place at the center of their concerns."

I created the term *Homo noeticus* in 1973, shortly after we organized IONS, to designate a more advanced form of humanity that I saw emerging around the planet, characterized primarily by a higher state of consciousness, a state beyond egocentric consciousness. As Canadian psychiatrist Richard M. Bucke put it so powerfully in his seminal 1901 book *Cosmic Consciousness*, "when we are in tune with a consciousness of the cosmos, we become members of a new species." Moreover, I saw the process of higher human development as essentially open to the entire race, democratically available to all people and intended so by God. Awakening to that potential for self-directed growth in body, mind, and spirit to a higher state of being was, I believed (and still do), the true and permanent solution to the many worldwide problems which we sought to address at IONS—problems collectively called the human condition. Acutely, palpably, I felt destiny working in me and all humanity, impelled by the awesome divine intelligence that had created the cosmos and everything in it. I therefore began communicating that understanding in order to help awaken my human family to its future. Homo noeticus seemed a useful term to convey that message. The message can be stated simply: human potential can change the human condition.

> The message can be stated simply: human potential can change the human condition.

Since then, the term Homo noeticus has been adopted approvingly by some. It has also been criticized as imprecise and unscientific by some, and as a poetic fantasy by others. I acknowledge that the term is scientifically imprecise. I am not a scientist—only a student of science. Nor am I a poet, although I appreciate the poet's sensibilities and vision. However, as I intended it, the term Homo noeticus is both quasi-scientific and quasi-poetic. It denotes a concept yet to be proven true, for which only time will tell; as such, one could say it is an untestable hypothesis and therefore not scientific. However, it also conveys an appealing image of the ideal future such as poets have offered, which may prove self-fulfilling; as such, one could say the term is useful and valuable because it points to the fact that vision is higher than reason in the ranking order of human faculties and can galvanize our attention into action where mere facts cannot.

An Interview with Noetic Scientist Marilyn Schlitz

The character Katherine Solomon is a composite of several people in the field of "Noetic Sciences," but she resembles no one more than Marilyn Schlitz, the current president of the Institute of Noetic Sciences (IONS) in Petaluma, California.

How does it feel to be the inspiration, at least in part, for one of the main characters in what may be the best-selling novel of all time?

It's the stuff that dreams are made of—if one dreams of such things. For me, it does feel like a dream. Out of the blue my colleagues and I have become part of the plot line in Dan Brown's new book. Still, I must confess, short of olive-colored skin, long hair, a wealthy family, and a crazy sociopath pursuing her, there are some exceptional similarities in our mutual bios.

Really? How so?

Both my father and my brother were 32nd-degree Masons and members of the Scottish Rite. I grew up wondering about the secret meetings for men only.

Photo by Kelly Durkin.

My father and my brother learned mysterious symbols that could not be shared with me, despite my many probing questions. My father wore the iconic Masonic ring, which was passed down to my brother after his death, just as it was in Katherine's family. As Noetic Scientists, Katherine and I share a mutual fascination with the powers and potentials of consciousness. We have both pursued careers well outside the mainstream and both live our work, as friends and family can attest.

Did Dan Brown know this? Did he ever contact you for information?

No, but after the book was published, we received a thoughtful note from him saying that he is a big fan of IONS, that he had hoped to give us a heads-up but could not due to the secrecy behind the book, and hoping we are enjoying the attention.

So are there any other parallels between you and the character Katherine Solomon?

Like Katherine, my career began at the ripe age of nineteen. And early on, my mentor was a neurophysiologist who introduced me to ancient Egyptian texts and modern scientific views of consciousness. As an undergraduate at Montieth College, Wayne State University, I read Newton, Ptolemy, Pythagoras, and Copernicus, as well as spiritualism, theosophy, parapsychology, and comparative religion. Like Katherine, I was looking for ways to broker a paradigm shift for our modern age.

I began as an experimental parapsychologist, studying the interface of mind and matter. I published my first paper on remote viewing in 1979; this attracted members of the CIA/DIA team doing classified work on psychic phenomena. Years later I gained security clearance through my work in the Cognitive Sciences Laboratory at SAIC, a large, government-sponsored research site where I conducted research on mind over matter. While my work was never classified directly, I can easily stretch my imagination to that of Katherine's fictional story—her research hidden deep in a web of classified intelligence.

Throughout the past three decades, I conducted laboratory-based and clinical studies involving distant intention, prayer, altered states of consciousness, contemplative practice, subtle energies, and healing. Like the Noetic Sciences program in *The Lost Symbol*, my experimental research has included studies of distant intention on living systems, including microorganisms, mice, and human physiology. My research on distant mental influences on living systems has been replicated in laboratories around the world, moving it beyond fiction and into peer review journals.

In the book Dan Brown combines the parapsychological research of several groups under the flag of "noetic science." What kinds of research does IONS itself focus on today?

We are delighted to see so many of our colleagues' work organized under Noetic Sciences. And we are also pleased that much of the research in the book is from, or in partnership with, IONS. Senior Scientist Dean Radin did the study on water crystals with Masaru Emoto that's mentioned in the book, and we are the fiscal and program sponsor for the Global Consciousness Project run by Roger Nelson.

At IONS, our programs are focused on understanding the interface of consciousness and science. We have organized our work into three principal program areas, including Consciousness and Healing, Extended Human Capacities, and Emerging Worldviews. We conduct and support basic science research, including beliefs, intentions, worldview, contemplative practices, and consciousness transformation. We do applications research to examine the health benefits (or not) of Noetic experiences and consciousness transformation practices, including an NIH-funded study of distant prayer and expectancy effects for patients undergoing surgery and multi-year studies of

> Focusing on human consciousness through the lens of science may well lead to major breakthroughs in our understanding of our human endeavor...

transformative training programs for homeless, at-risk moms and people seeking stress reduction.

We translate our findings into educational programs for lifelong learning, for health and healing practitioners, and for students through our new worldview literacy program for students in grades K to 12. We are also a membership and communications organization that seeks to connect people and seed ideas and actions to promote positive personal and collective transformation. Our website, noetics.org, is a place for everyone and anyone who wants to learn more about us...not a hidden treasure, but something in plain view for everyone.

How do you respond to Dan Brown's characterization of noetics research as "so advanced that it no longer resemble[s] science"?
At the time of Descartes, a political deal was struck between scientists and the church. Science studied the body, the church was left with the inner

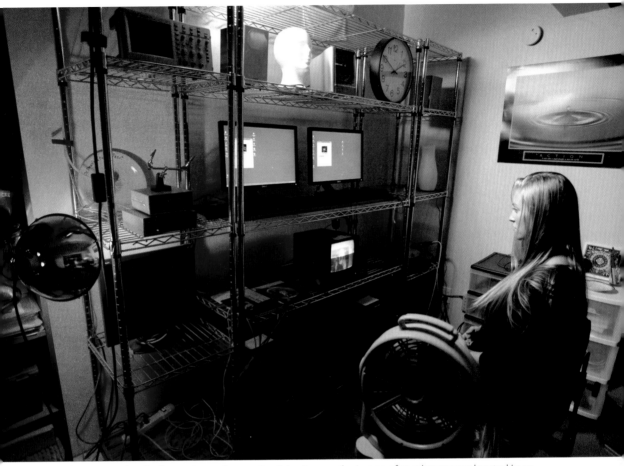

A volunteer in a "staring" experiment focuses her intention on the image of another person located in an electrically shielded experimental chamber. *Photo by Kelly Durkin*

dimensions. We are still living in the legacy of this deal. So it is fair to say that science has neglected consciousness, at the very least. At the more extreme level, science has developed a worldview that assumes the physical, objective aspects of reality are the only valid domains for scientific inquiry. Just asking the scientific question, can prayer heal from a distance, is considered very radical. There are very clearly paradigm wars that limit the scope of "acceptable" science and the flow of funding for ideas that don't fit into mainstream materialism.

Do you feel that Brown has oversold the potential of your work by saying that the findings of noetic science contains "the most transformative scientific revelations in human history"?

I agree with Dan about the implications of our work and appreciate the way in which he has been able to translate them through a compelling and dramatic work of fiction. I think it is true that focusing on human consciousness through the lens of science may well lead to major breakthroughs in our understanding of our human endeavor and to creative new solutions to age-old problems. Of course, there have been other major paradigm shifts in history, but we are pleased to be a participant in a current period of profound transformation that has the potential to help create a more just, compassionate, and sustainable world.

Dan Brown places the noetic sciences lab of his character at the Smithsonian Institution, specifically at their Museum Support Center. Do you think the kind of research you do will ever be acceptable enough in the eyes the scientific establishment for this kind of work to be conducted at such an august institution?

Well, I have lectured at the Smithsonian, as well as the United Nations, and Harvard and Stanford Universities. My colleagues and I have also been consultants for many major hospitals and medical systems. While we are not mainstream, our work is timely and relevant. Through our research, education, and membership programs, we are helping people navigate through this time of destabilization and to envision a new worldview that combines insights from the world's wisdom traditions with the rigor and discernment of modern science.

The PEAR Laboratory   *by Brenda Dunne*

In The Lost Symbol, *the character of Katherine Solomon appears to be based on noetic scientist Marilyn Schlitz, and that of Trish Dunne on Brenda Dunne, the cofounder and manager of the Princeton Engineering Anomalies Research laboratory, which Dan Brown mentions briefly in the book.*

The Princeton Engineering Anomalies Research (PEAR) program was established in 1979 in the School of Engineering and Applied Science at Princeton University under the direction of Professor Robert Jahn, a distinguished aerospace engineer who served as dean of the engineering school for fifteen years. Its primary purpose was the systematic study of a selection of anomalous consciousness-related physical phenomena of potential pertinence to contemporary and future information-processing technologies.

As its title implies, PEAR was an academically based, engineering oriented, rigorously scientific research enterprise, aspiring to increasing basic understanding of the fundamental processes contributing to the anomalous effects, their implications for various scholarly disciplines, and their potential practical applications. From its inception and

Trying to influence the turbulent dynamic characteristics of an illuminated fountain. *Photo courtesy of ICRL, Inc.*

throughout its subsequent twenty-eight-year history, the program conducted many millions of experimental trials under controlled scientific conditions, producing persuasive evidence that human consciousness is capable of influencing random physical processes and accessing

Attempting to alter the damping rate of a large crystal pendulum. *Photo courtesy of ICRL, Inc.*

information about remote geographical locations, without recourse to any known physical mechanisms.

We proposed complementary theoretical models to enable better understanding of the role of consciousness in the establishment of physical reality. Results of this extensive research program have been presented in some fifty archival publications, and in the book, *Margins of Reality*, originally published by Harcourt Brace Jovanovich in 1987 and recently reissued by ICRL Press.

PEAR has now incorporated its former and future operations into the broader venues of the International Consciousness Research Laboratories (ICRL), a not-for-profit organization, and Psyleron, Inc., a company that develops products and deploys broadly ranging intellectual property that enable ongoing research and public exploration of mind-matter effects.

The purpose of ICRL is to extend the work of PEAR into a broader range of inquiry through basic research, educational outreach, and pragmatic applications; to encourage a new generation of creative investigators to expand the boundaries of scientific understanding; and to strengthen the foundations of science by reclaiming its spiritual heritage.

Is the Global Mind Real?   *By Roger Nelson*

Roger Nelson is a psychologist and the director of the Global Consciousness Project, which Dan Brown alludes to in his book. The project's website at noosphere.princeton.edu hosts complete information about the history, technology, and methods of the project, as well as free public access to the database. The following is excerpted from an article that appeared in a magazine called EdgeScience, October 2009, available at http://www.scientificexploration.org.

History changed course in late 2001, when the world watched in shock and horror as the World Trade Towers collapsed, destroyed by passenger planes turned into bombs by terrorists. It was a long moment of profound emotional sharing across the globe, with shock and fear turning to anguish and ultimately to compassion. In the midst of the tragedy many of us could see signs of humanity coming together as one. That was not to be, sadly. But for a moment, there was a powerful convergence of thought and emotion across the world that registered clearly in data from the Global Consciousness Project. Could this scientific instrument have picked up our coherence, the signature of a global mind startled awake by the intense synchronized activity of our local minds?

The Global Consciousness Project, or GCP, is an international collaboration of scientists running an instrument designed to capture possible effects

A week of GCP data, with the normally random walk changing radically on September 11, 2001. Beginning a little before the terrorist attacks, the data show a persistent trend for 50 hours, correlated with the shared emotions of millions of people reacting to the tragedy.

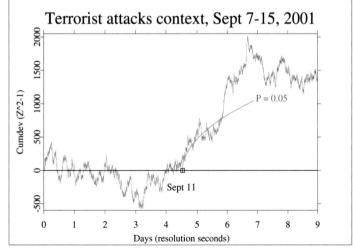

131

of shared consciousness, much in the way that laboratory experiments have shown effects of intention on sensitive electronic devices that generate random numbers. In the lab, a person tries to change the behavior of a Random Number Generator (or RNG, which is a physical device, not a computer program) to produce smaller or larger numbers—the equivalent of flipping a coin and getting an excess of heads—just by wishing or willing the change. The experiments show that human intention can induce small, but significant changes in the output of an RNG. When we take the same instruments into the field, we find they also respond to special moments of

Composite result for 280 independent tests of the hypothesis that structure will be found in the array of random data correlated with major global events. The results are well beyond expectations (black line).

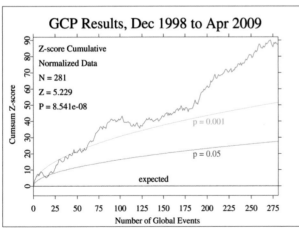

group consciousness produced by shared experience in rituals and ceremonies, or inspired by great music or intense meetings of mind.

The GCP instrument is a network of stations around the world where random data are collected. It uses the same technology as the lab and field experiments, and asks the natural question: Is there non-random structure in the data when great events occur?

We began collecting data in August 1998, prepared to create a history of parallel random sequences that could be correlated with the history of major events on the world stage. We knew some good questions to ask. Might there be something interconnecting us all, though we are unaware of it? Of course the sages have been saying so forever, but could we get evidence of it "on paper" in a scientific sense? Could the earth have some holistic response to what happens to her populations of living beings? Would we notice a global mind?

With contributions from more than a hundred scientists, engineers, artists, and friends around the world, the project grew in a few years to about 65 sites hosting eggs (we called our RNG devices EGGS, for ElectroGaiaGram), each reporting data continuously, in locations from Alaska to Fiji, on all populated continents and in nearly every time zone. The result is a research instrument built as a distributed network of devices, which apparently can be affected by human consciousness under special conditions. Its purpose is to gather evidence and study indications of the subtle reach of consciousness in the physical world on a global scale. The general hypothesis we propose is that the array of random data from the GCP instrument will become non-random during "global events." We predict departures from expectation when there is a widespread, profound sharing of mental and emotional responses.

The proposition has been tested in a series of rigorously specified formal hypothesis tests. We have registered more than 280 formal experiments as of early 2009. Combined across events, the GCP effect implies that the behavior of RNGs separated by global distances becomes correlated during events of importance to humans. This is a profoundly mysterious outcome that stretches our scientific imaginations. The results confirm our hypothesis in about two thirds of the cases and show significance for about 20 percent of the events (5 percent would be expected by chance). The overall statistics for the project indicate odds of about 1 in 20 million that the correlation of our data with global events is merely a chance fluctuation, and we can exclude mundane explanations such as electromagnetic radiation, excessive strain on the power grid, or mobile phone use. Though this can't be taken as proof of an awakening global consciousness, it is suggestive. In any case the results definitely present challenging conundrums for physics and psychology.

We don't yet know how to explain the correlations between events of importance to humans and the GCP data, but they are quite clear. They suggest something akin to the image held in almost all cultures of a unity or oneness, an interconnection that is fundamental to life. Our efforts to understand these complex data may contribute insight into the role of mind as a creative force in the world, able to manifest intentions and capable of conscious evolution.

INSIDE THE ENTANGLED GLOBAL MIND *By Dean Radin*

Dean Radin is Senior Scientist at the Institute of Noetic Sciences and the author of Entangled Minds: Extrasensory Experiences in a Quantum Reality, *from which this excerpt is drawn.*

To see the world in a grain of sand
And a heaven in a wild flower,
Hold infinity in the palm of your hand
And eternity in an hour.

—WILLIAM BLAKE

Blake's poem hints at how an entangled mind might perceive the world. My guess is that Blake's description points in the right direction for an understanding of psi. At a level of reality deeper than the ordinary senses can grasp, our brains and minds are in intimate communion with the universe. It's as though we live in a gigantic bowl of clear Jell-O. Every wiggle every movement, event, and thought within that medium is felt throughout the entire bowl. Except that this particular form of Jell-O is a rather peculiar medium, in that it's not localized in the usual way, nor is it squishy like ordinary Jell-O. It extends beyond the bounds of ordinary spacetime, and it's not even a substance in the usual sense of that word.

Because of this "nonlocal Jell-O" in which we are embedded, we can get glimpses of information about other people's minds, distant objects, or the future or past. We get this information not through the ordinary senses, and not because signals from those other minds and objects travel to our brain, but because at some level our mind/brain is already coexistent with other people's minds, distant objects, and everything else. To navigate through this space, we use attention and intention. From this perspective, psychic experiences are reframed not as mysterious "powers of the mind" but as momentary glimpses of the entangled fabric of reality.

Maybe psi doesn't involve information transfer at all. Maybe it's purely relational and manifests only as correlations. To explain this in more detail, let's assume that our bodies, minds, and brains are entangled in a holistic universe. It is not necessary to assume that the mind is fundamentally different from the brain, or the even more radical notion that reality is created by consciousness. It is only necessary to imagine that the mind/brain behaves as a quantum object. Imagine that our mind/brain is sensitive to the dynamic state of the entire universe. There are an astounding number of events we can potentially react to, but the vast majority of them can be regarded as background noise. Other than where your body is, you might be interested in perhaps ten other locations or events within the universe at any given moment, all of them relatively close to you in spacetime.

Some portion of your unconscious mind pays attention to those selected locations at all times. Like suddenly hearing your name mentioned at a noisy cocktail party, you become consciously aware of items of interest through your unconscious scanning ability. Most of your conscious awareness is heavily driven by sensory inputs. That sensory-bound brain state is also entangled and influenced by the rest of the universe, but its local effects are so much stronger and immediate than our "background" awareness that only on rare occasions are we aware of its entangled nature. A few gifted individuals are able to direct their conscious awareness at will to surf through the entangled unconscious, but even they have trouble maintaining that state for long, as the act of seeing disturbs that which is seen. For the rest of us, we have to rely on our unconscious mind(s) to pay attention to those fleeting events of interest.

On occasion, if a distant loved one is in danger, the part of your unconscious that has been attending to the environment alerts your conscious self. You might experience this alert as a gut feeling, as an odd sense of something meaningful afoot, or your imagination might be activated and you might perceive a fleeting vision of your loved one. On extraordinary occasions, you might obtain a veridical sense of what is happening somewhere, or some-when, else.

If you later learned that indeed your loved one was in danger, or wished to communicate with you, then you'd call this a case of spooky telepathy. It would appear to be a form of information transfer, but in fact it would be a pure correlation. That is, within a holistic medium we are always connected. No information transfer need take place because there are no separate parts. Navigation through this reality occurs through our attention, and nonsensory perception takes place through our activated memory and imagination.

FINDING THE LOST SYMBOLS IN WASHINGTON, D.C.

The George Washington Masonic Memorial

L ocated on Shuters Hill in Alexandria, this is one building that is not hiding from anyone!

It is a Masonic tradition to build temples on hilltops or mountains, and this one is built where Thomas Jefferson proposed to build the Capitol.

Modeled after the Lighthouse of Alexandria, Egypt, the Memorial stands ten stories tall, capped with a pyramid and flame-like finial. If you've ever flown into Washington, D.C., at night, and looked out the window you've probably seen it.

The ground-breaking ceremony for the Memorial took place on June 5, 1922. On November 1, 1923, President Calvin Coolidge and former President and Chief Justice William H. Taft were among those in attendance when the cornerstone was dedicated. Since no money was borrowed to finance its construction, and the country went into the Great Depression, progress was slow. The building was finally dedicated on May 12, 1932, with President Herbert Hoover in attendance, and the interior completed in 1970.

The Ark of the Covenant.

Unlike other Masonic Lodges, the George Washington houses exhibits from various different Masonic bodies, including Scottish and York Rites, Shriners, and Tall Cedars of Lebanon.

The building is open to the public, visitors (Masons and non-Masons) are welcome, and tours are conducted regularly.

George Washington Laying the Cornerstone of the National Capitol, September 18, 1793 by Allyn Cox

In addition to his work on display in the George Washington Masonic Memorial, Allyn Cox also completed the frieze in the Capitol Rotunda, which had been begun by Constantino Brumidi, and a depiction of the first moon landing, which is in the Brumidi Corridors.

Those in attendance at this ceremony from left to right are:
Senator Robert Young of Virginia; Archibald Dobbin of Baltimore; Ferdinando Fairfax of Virginia; Benjamin Tasker Dulany of Alexandria; Col. Dennis Ramsay and Col. William Payne, both of Alexandria Lodge No. 22; David Stuart, District Commissioner; Daniel Carroll, District Commissioner; James Hoban, Architect, Federal Lodge No. 15, Maryland; Stephen Hallate, Architect; Thomas Johnson, District Commissioner; George Washington; Joseph Clark, Annapolis Lodge No. 12; Dr. Elisha Cullen Dick, Alexandria Lodge No. 22; Clotworthy Stephenson, Federal Lodge No. 15, Maryland; Valentine Reintzel, Georgetown Lodge No. 9; Colin Williamson, Federal Lodge No. 15, Maryland; James Thompson; Georgetown Lodge No. 9; Martha Washington; Eleanor Parke Custis, wife of Commissioner Johnson.

CHAPTER FIVE
Decoding The Lost Symbol

Masonic Tracing Board, ca. 1820, attributed to John Ritto
Penniman (1782–1841) Boston, Massachusetts. Oil on canvas.
Scottish Rite Masonic Museum and Library, 89.76.
Photography by David Boh

Solving the Codes on the Cover of The Lost Symbol *by Greg Taylor*

In late 2003 Greg Taylor learned that the dust jacket of Dan Brown's The Da Vinci Code *contained a number of curious "anomalies"—map co-ordinates in "mirror writing," bolded letters hiding odd messages, and more. Then, in an interview, Dan Brown announced that clues about the sequel to* The Da Vinci Code *were hidden on the cover of his bestselling book. By solving these puzzles and ciphers, Taylor was able to write a complete primer on Brown's as-yet unpublished book in late 2004. In* Da Vinci in America, *Taylor provided background information on many of the topics that he surmised would be in the new book—quite correctly as it turns out. When the cover artwork for* The Lost Symbol *was released in July 2009, prior to the book's publication in September, Taylor and fellow symbologists got back to work. You'll need to have the cover of* The Lost Symbol *on hand to follow his decipherment.*

The cover of *The Lost Symbol* features a torn "parchment" theme similar to the cover of *The Da Vinci Code,* though with Capitol Hill in Washington, D.C., as the focus rather than the Mona Lisa, and the Washington Monument hidden away in the keyhole on the spine. Also prominent is a wax seal emblazoned with a double-headed eagle—a direct confirmation that Freemasonry, in particular Scottish Rite Masonry—plays a major role in the new book.

The 33 in the center of the triangle on the seal comes from the fact that there are 33 "degrees" (levels of initiation) in Scottish Rite Freemasonry. As it turns out, its presence on the cover is just the tip of the iceberg—Dan Brown seems to have used the number as an "in-joke" throughout *The Lost Symbol*: the introduction begins at 8:33 p.m., there are 133 chapters, and on page 333 there are no less than twelve references to it, all in a section that Brown introduces by stating that "the tradition of numerology hailed the number 33 as the highest of

Melencolia I by Albrect Dürer.

all the Master Numbers." If that wasn't enough, the three numbers making up the release date of the book, 09/15/09, add up to the number 33!

Not so noticeable on the cover though are various symbols imprinted on the parchment, taken from astrology, alchemy, and other esoteric fields—all setting the perfect vibe for the cover of a Dan Brown novel. But on closer inspection, something else becomes apparent. Once again, Dan Brown has hidden some codes on the cover of his latest book.

First, randomly spread between the front cover and the spine, are letter-number combinations. Above the R of Brown" we find "B1." On the left, above "a novel," there is another: "C2." And also, on the far right of the cover, is "J5." Meanwhile, at the top left of the spine we find "E8," and just above the keyhole at the bottom of the spine is "H5."

So the "pre-released" front cover and spine displayed the following codes: B1, C2, E8, H5, and J5. However, the alphabetical nature of the letter-number combinations—B, C, E, H, and J—suggests that at least five more are missing: A#, D#, F#, G# and I# (which would complete the first ten letters in the alphabet, A to J). But without the back cover, the code was unbreakable. Or was it?

A number of very smart people who were working on cracking this code noted that in the previous DaVinci Code WebQuest, an online game associated with the book, participants were asked to call the numbers (212) 782-9920 and (212) 782-9932. These numbers seemed to be part of a phone number allocation to publisher Random House in New York, whose main number is (212) 782-9000, with the first seven numbers (212-782-9###) being common to all their numbers.

The reader has probably already noted that the new cover codes fit this template perfectly. Arranging the five known codes in alphabetical order to fit the phone number template (ABC-DEF-GHIJ), and substituting the corresponding number for the letter, gives us five of the ten digits in the phone number: #12-#8#-#5#5. Using the known Random House numbers as a base allowed some educated guesses at four of the other letter-number combinations: A2, D7, F2, and G9. This just left I# as the only unknown (212-782-95#5); ten possibilities, easy enough to solve through brute force if someone were willing to call each one.

It turns out that a number of people did, but they were met with Random House offices and answering machines—but no competition hotline. This despite confirmation from a newly activated "Symbol Quest" on Dan Brown's website for *The Lost Symbol*—in which the participant had to answer 33 consecutive riddles based on various symbols—which, once completed, featured a recording of Dan Brown stating that there were codes on the cover of *The Lost Symbol* that would decode to a telephone number, through which 33 lucky contestants would receive a signed copy of his new book.

As it turns out, the decoding was correct—but it was just done too quickly! Random House had not "turned on" the competition phone response at such an early stage. Persistent callers found late on the 14th of September (the day before publication of *The Lost Symbol*) that the competition had gone "live" on the number (212) 782-9515. A new message was available, from Brown's editor Jason Kaufman, asking contestants to submit an email to a certain address; if they were one of the first 33, they would receive a signed copy of *The Lost Symbol*.

Once released on September 15, the back cover of the book confirmed the decoding: the letter-number combinations A2, D7, F2, G9, and I1 are all found there. It is likely then that anybody who solved the phone number code *after* buying the book (and seeing the back cover) would have been too late—the first 33 emails were probably received before *The Lost Symbol* even hit bookstore shelves.

But that's not all. There are more codes on the cover than just these letter-number combinations. On the front cover, just on the inside and outside of the left hand side of the faint circle surrounding the Scottish Rite seal, are two sets of numbers:

Outside: 22-65-22-97-27
Inside: 22-23-44-1-133-97-65-44

At first glance, the most notable aspect of this number sequence is the non-random appearance of repeated numbers: 22, 44, 97, and 65. This suggests that the numbers are to be substituted for letters in two words, with 22, 44, 97, and 65 being repeated letters. Further, this number sequence echos a code found on the back page of Dan Brown's 1998 book *Digital Fortress*: 128-10-93-85-10-128-98-112-6-6-25-126-39-1-68-78. The solution in that case was that each of the numbers referred to a chapter, and taking the first letter of each of those chapters yielded (after using a further decipher with a "Caesar Box") the secret message "We are watching you." If this new code used the same deciphering method, it seemed that it could not be solved until the book was published and the first letters of the various chapters were known.

Once again, however, brute force deciphering techniques came to the fore. Assuming that the numbers do indeed stand for letters, substitution analysis can be done by taking into consideration the repeated "letters," as well as regular English-language use of certain letter combinations and their positions within words. This narrows down the number of possible words that can be represented significantly. Some people are good enough (and have enough spare time!) to do this with paper and pencil, but in the modern age can be done more efficiently by using a computer. For example, by converting the number sequence into an equivalent letter sequence—preserving the sequence and repeated elements (e.g. ABACD AEFGHCBF)—we can use an online tool such as "Decrypto" (http://www. blisstonia.com/software/WebDecrypto/ index.php) to do the work for us.

In just 0.022 seconds Decrypto returns only 15 possible word combinations, and for anybody familiar with the content of *The Lost Symbol*, one in particular stands out: "POPES PANTHEON." John Russell Pope is famous for being the architect behind a number of prominent buildings in Washington, D.C., including the National Archives, the Jefferson Memorial, the West Building of the National Gallery of Art, and the Scottish Rite's "House of the Temple." Furthermore, some of these buildings were influenced by the architecture of the Pantheon in Rome, perhaps most prominently the Jefferson Memorial.

Again, this pre-publication solution was confirmed once *The Lost Symbol* was released. Just as surmised, each number pointed to a chapter, from which the first letter was taken and substituted into the sequence. For example, Chapter 22 begins with "Pacing," Chapter 65 "Once," Chapter 97 "Eight," Chapter 27 "Systems." Using the first letters of each of these four chapters, and substituting into the first five numbers of the sequence ('22'/'P' is repeated at positions 1 and 3) we get "POPES." Continuing this with the second sequence gives "PANTHEON." Not the easiest way to decipher the codes obviously, but you still have to admire the ingenuity of the brute force deciphering before publication! Further confirmation that this code points to the Jefferson Memorial comes in the text of *The Lost Symbol*, with Brown twice referencing the monument as being based on the Pantheon.

However, two other codes could only be deciphered once *The Lost Symbol* had been released—simply because they are only on the back cover. Most prominent is the "Masonic Cipher" (also known as the "Pigpen Cipher") written just inside the verticals of the decorative frame. To "read" the symbols in the correct orientation, rotate the back cover 90 degrees clockwise.

Though this is a well-known cipher method and could be decoded without too much help, Dan Brown offers the actual key on page 197 of *The Lost Symbol* (describing it as "almost infantile"). Each symbol is actually the uniquely shaped enclosure of each letter's position in the "pigpen" grid.

So to start, we have the top-left grid square corresponding to "A." The next two are the top right grid-squares featuring a dot: "L"; so the first word is "ALL." Continuing on with this deciphering method reveals the statement "ALL GREAT TRUTHS BEGIN AS BLASPHEMIES," which is a quote from the Irish playwright George Bernard Shaw, and which applies neatly to many

Masonic Tracing Board, 1818. Jonas Prentiss (1777–1832) West Cambridge, Massachusetts. Oil on canvas *Scottish Rite Masonic Museum and Library, Gift of Hiram Lodge, A.F. & A.M., Arlington, Massachusetts, 91.048. Photography by David Bohl*

of the topics Dan Brown discusses in his novels.

Last then, perhaps the most novel cipher technique used by Dan Brown in *The Lost Symbol* is the grid square that is decoded using the number layout in the "Magic Square of Jupiter" found in the 1514 engraving *Melencolia* I by the Renaissance master Albrecht Dürer. As Dan Brown discusses, adding each row, column, diagonal in this Magic Square gives a total of 34 (what a shame that wasn't 33!).

On the back cover we find another 4 x 4 square, beginning and ending with a "Y." While again this jumble of letters could be brute-forced if necessary (it baffles Nola Kaye in *The Lost Symbol*, but in reality no CIA analyst would have any trouble with it at all), Dan Brown explains all in the pages of the book. All that is required is to navigate the grid squares in numerical sequence: in Dürer's square, the number "1" is at bottom right, so in the corresponding square in the cover cipher we find a "Y." Number "2" is third square in the top row, corresponding to "O" in cipher square; "3" equals "U," "4" is "R." Continuing on, the entire message is revealed: "YOUR MIND IS THE KEY," which relates well to Ancient Mysteries and Noetic Science content of *The Lost Symbol*.

But do these phrases have further meaning? It might be worth remember-ing that the codes on the cover of *The Da Vinci Code* pointed at topics in Dan Brown's next book, *The Lost Symbol*—although, given that they allowed me to preempt him by five years, this may be a strategy that he and his publishers no longer wish to pursue!

There is one final thing worth not-ing about the cover, and that is that Dan Brown has said that there are *five* hid-den messages on the cover. Thus far I've mentioned four—so what is the final message? It may simply be the lines mirrored at the top and bottom of the decorative text frame on the back cover, the well-known Hermetic axiom: "AS ABOVE SO BELOW." But this hardly seems to be a hidden code. Could it then simply reveal a method for solving a fifth code? Or perhaps a final message is hidden somewhere among the vari-ous symbols found on the cover? Why not grab your copy and see what you can find—there may be something still wait-ing to be discovered. And keep your eye on my Dan Brown–related website The Cryptex (http://www.thecryptex.com) for further updates.

Chamber of Reflection

Jess Maghan, 40 Fathers: The Search for Father in Oneself.
Historian, Solar Lodge No. 131, A. F. & A. M. CT.

"A man who has undertaken a thing after mature reflection seldom turns back."

—Mackey's *Encyclopedia of Freemasonry**

In many ways the Chamber of Reflection is a starting point on the journey into Free Masonry. It is an anteroom, located at the threshold of the Lodge, where a candidate reflects on and affirms his desire to become an "entered apprentice." Primarily, this is the entry point for witnessing his integrity of character, sense of responsibility, and capacity for perseverance and duty. The candidate is blindfolded, robed, and prepared to enter the Lodge for presentation to the Worshipful Master, the Officers, and his future Brother Masons. In the process, his blindfold will be removed, giving him his first exposure to the pure light of Masonry. Within the Lodge he will receive basic guidance and counseling on the rich history of Masonry and its code of conduct and guiding symbols of the Craft. In future years, as he continues his journey, he may choose to affiliate with The Ancient Arabic Order of the Nobles of the Mystic Shrine, Knights of Templar, or make the quest for the highest degrees of Masonry, which will require a more arduous and intrusive Chamber of Reflection on the purity of heart and soul as epitomized in the alchemic symbolism of Masonry. This higher path will require absolute perseverance and a vigilance of personal reflection based on the metaphors of one's life from the cradle to the grave, the mystery of time, and its transforming stages of maturity and purity of a spiritual countenance. "True initiation is an individual process. Nobody can transform a man but himself. Others may guide and help, but ultimately, the process is an inside job. The individual alone is the only one who can perform the great work. The Chamber of Reflection truly epitomizes this process."**

* Mackey, Albert, and Charles T. McClenachan, *Encyclopedia of Freemasonry* [Rev. eds. by Edward Hawkins and William Hughan, vol. 1 & 2].

**W. Bro. Helio L. Da Costa Jr., *The Chamber of Reflection*, presented at the Vancouver Grand Masonic Day, 10/16/1999; 1871–2009 Grand Lodge of British Columbia and Yukon, A. F. & A. M. (08/02/2001, freemasonry.bcy.ca/texts/gmd1999/pondering.html).

The Double-Headed Phoenix   by Loren Coleman

Loren Coleman is an expert in twilight language, those "coded words," "name games," and "number coincidences" found in the news, in history, and in fiction. He explores the subject in two books, Mysterious America *and* The Copycat Effect, *and on his Twilight Language blog at http://copycat effect.blogspot.com.*

Dan Brown writes about various signs, locations, numbers, and symbols that are hidden in plain view. But it is perhaps what Brown himself hides within the pages of his new book and does not fully reveal that should interest us the most. Indeed, Brown appears to be teasing us throughout his fast-paced adventure with an important occult symbol he does not explain in any great detail, although he has embedded it at a symbolic numerical level throughout his book. Are we being played with, even as we read this book, by a master symbologist, named Dan Brown?

As I was reading the book, I noticed Brown mentioning, sometimes quite jarringly, the "double-headed phoenix." The double-headed phoenix is noted as a tattoo on the chest of Mal'akh (5 times), on Peter Solomon's Masonic ring (5 times), on the seal to the capstone's wrapping, on a Masonic "diploma," and on a medallion. I do not think it is a coincidence that Brown mentions this special kind of phoenix specifically 13 times within the book. (Although in one other appearance, Brown mentions a "phoenix" in a dream, and in another instance, Brown writes of a "two-headed bird" without using the word "*phoenix*.")

Everyone is familiar with the idea of the Phoenix, a bird rising from the aftermath of a fire, as symbolizing rebirth. The word *phoenix* comes from the Ancient Greek work Φοίνιξ, *phoenix*, said to be a sacred firebird with origins in several ancient mythologies. The Egyptians linked the phoenix to their sun god Ra and the city Heliopolis, well known for its obelisks. In China, the leader of the birds, the Fenghuang, is a mirror of the phoenix. The phoenix is also apparent as the Garuda, the bird of the Hindi god Vishnu.

So commonplace is the symbol of the Phoenix today that the City of Portland, Maine, where I live, has adopted on the city seal a phoenix rising out of ashes, which aligns with its motto, *Resurgam*, Latin for "I will rise again," in reference to Portland's recovery from devastating fires. Most noteworthy is the massive fire that occurred during a July 4, 1866, celebration, which left 10,000 homeless and destroyed the city's entire financial and trade center.

Even a superficial reading of *The Lost Symbol* rather obviously reveals that being "reborn" is important to such characters as Katherine Solomon, who understands how the discoveries of her noetic science experiments could

bring about the "brave new world," and to Mal'akh who reinvents himself after being shot by Peter Solomon.

But there's more to the double-headed phoenix for Dan Brown. It is, as he states, of great significance to the Freemasons. It is a key to the hidden mysteries, and it is associated, especially for those caught in the quicksand of conspiracy theories, with sinister forces and Lucifer reborn.

Modern Masons unaware of their own histories may feel that Dan Brown has made a big mistake by bringing up a "double-headed phoenix," when modern

Double-headed eagle on the door of Scottish Rite Temple, Washington, DC.

Brothers in the Craft understand it as a "double-headed eagle" in all of their contemporary materials. But no leveling of the square through Masonic "hoodwinking" shall submerge the bird's true identity as the phoenix, which evolved into bird very familiar to Americans, the eagle.

The famed 33rd-degree Masonic author Manly P. Hall penned the following critical observation in his book, *The Lost Keys of Freemasonry*: "These were the immortals to whom the term *phoenix* was applied, and their symbol was the mysterious two-headed bird, now called an eagle, a familiar and little understood Masonic emblem."

In *The Phoenix: An Illustrated Review of Occultism and Philosophy*, Hall took a closer look at the subject: "Among the ancients a fabulous bird called the Phoenix is described by early writers...in size and shape it resembles the eagle....The Phoenix, it is said, lives for 500 years, and at its death its body opens and the new born Phoenix emerges. Because of this symbolism, the Phoenix is generally regarded as representing immortality and resurrection....The Phoenix is one sign of the secret orders of the ancient world and of the initiate of those orders, for it was common to refer to one who

had been accepted into the temples as a man twice-born, or reborn. Wisdom confers a new life, and those who become wise are born again."

And another Masonic writer, R. Swinburne Clymer, notes in *The Mysteries of Osiris*: "When they [the ancients] desired to express the renewal, or beginning, of the year, they represented it in the form of a door-keeper. It could easily be distinguished by the attributes of a key....At times, they gave it two heads, back to back....In time, this [back-to-back key symbol] became the double-headed Eagle of symbolic Masonry."

The double-headed phoenix has evolved into the eagle that's on the back of that dollar bill in your wallet or purse. You know, the one that has 13 arrows in its talons on the Masonic Great Seal. America is the transformation of outer reality as symbolized by the double-headed phoenix, the meeting of East and West, and ultimately the final stages of the alchemical processes that the Ancients wished to see occur.

What Dan Brown none too subtly reinforces with his 13 "double-headed phoenix" are the hidden references to the rebirth of the Masonic spirit in the founding of America.

Magic Squares

By Clifford A. Pickover

Clifford A. Pickover received his Ph.D. from Yale University and is the author of more than forty books on science, mathematics, art, and religion. His books include The Math Book, Archimedes to Hawking, *and* The Zen of Magic Squares, Circles and Stars. *His website is pickover.com.*

Dan Brown's talent for storytelling—replete with secret codes, history, and intrigue—is brought to the forefront in his novel *The Lost Symbol.* In fact, two famous number arrays called *magic squares* play a key role in the novel and help the protagonists decode a cryptic message.

Legends suggest that magic squares originated in China and were first mentioned in a manuscript from the time of Empery Yu, around 2200 B.C. Imagine a number array with *N* rows and *N* columns. A *magic square* consists of N^2 boxes, called *cells*, filled with integers that are all different. The sums of the numbers in the horizontal rows, vertical columns, and main diagonals are all equal. According to the ancient legend, Emperor Yu discovered the magic square while walking along the Lo River (or Yellow River) where he stumbled upon

a mystical turtle crawling on the riverbank. To Yu's amazement, the number and arrangement of spots on the turtle's back corresponded to a magic square.

If the integers in a magic square are the consecutive numbers from 1 to N^2, the square is said to be of the *N*th order, and the *magic number*—or sum of each row, column, or diagonal—is a constant equal to $N(N^2+1)/2$. Dan Brown features the most famous 4 × 4 magic square in history, created by Renaissance artist Albrecht Dürer (1471–1528), in 1514:

Note that the two central numbers in the bottom row read "1514," the year of its construction. The rows, columns, and main diagonals sum to 34. In addition, 34 is the sum of the numbers of the corner squares (16 + 13 + 4 + 1) and of the central 2 × 2 square (10 + 11 + 6 + 7). Interestingly, as far back as 1693, the 880 different fourth-order magic squares by Bernard Frénicle de Bessy (1602–1675), an eminent amateur French mathematician and one of the leading magic square researchers of all time, were published posthumously in *Des quassez ou tables magiques.*

My favorite ancient European magic square is, in fact, the Dürer magic square featured in Dan Brown's novel. It is drawn in the upper right-hand column of Dürer's etching *Melencolia I.* Dürer included a variety of small details in the etching that have confounded scholars for centuries. We seem to see the figure of a brooding genius sitting amid her uncompleted tasks. There are scattered tools, flowing sands in the glass, the magic square beneath the bell, the swaying balance. Scholars believe that the etching shows the insufficiency of human knowledge in attaining heavenly wisdom, or in penetrating the secrets of nature. Renaissance astrologers linked fourth-order magic squares to Jupiter, and these

52	61	4	13	20	29	36	45
14	3	62	51	46	35	30	19
53	60	5	12	21	28	37	44
11	6	59	54	43	38	27	22
55	58	7	10	23	26	39	42
9	8	57	56	41	40	25	24
50	63	2	15	18	31	34	47
16	1	64	49	48	33	32	17

squares were believed to combat melancholy (which was Saturnian in origin). Perhaps this explains the presence of the square in Dürer's engraving.

We've come a long way from the simplest 3 × 3 magic squares venerated by civilizations of almost every period and continent—from the Mayan Indians to the Hasua people of Africa. Today, mathematicians study these magic objects in high dimensions, for example in the form of 4-dimensional hypercubes that have magic sums within all appropriate directions.

Even the famous eighteenth-century American Benjamin Franklin (1706–1790) was fascinated by magic squares, although he once considered them a waste of time. Franklin wrote that "it was perhaps a mark of the good sense of our mathematicians that they would not spend their time in things that were merely *difficiles nuage,* incapable of any useful application." But he then admitted to having carefully studied and composed some amazing magic squares, even going as far to declare one of his squares "the most magically magical of any magic square ever made by any magician."

The Franklin 8 × 8 magic square plays a central role in *The Lost Symbol*. The first historical mention of the square is in 1769, in Franklin's letter to a colleague.

This magic square is filled with wondrous symmetries, some of which Ben Franklin was probably not aware. Each row and column of the square has a sum of 260. Half of each row or column sums to half of 260. In addition, each of the "bent rows" has the sum 260. (See gray shaded squares for two examples of "bent rows," see the thickly outlined squares for an example of a "broken bent row" [14 + 61 + 64 + 15 + 18 + 33 + 36 + 19], which also sums to 260.) Numerous other symmetries can be found: For example, the four corner numbers with the four middle numbers add up to 260. The sum of the numbers in any 2 × 2 sub-square is 130, and the sum of any four numbers that are arranged equidistant from the center of the square also equals 130. When converted to binary numbers even more startling symmetries are found. Alas, despite all the marvelous symmetries, the main diagonals don't

each sum to 260, so this square does not strictly qualify as a magic square, according to the common definition that includes the diagonal sums. If we closely examine Dan Brown's explanation in *The Lost Symbol*, it appears that he was not fully aware of this intriguing flaw in the Franklin square.

We do not know what method Franklin used to construct his squares. Many people have tried to crack the secret. Although Franklin claimed he could generate the squares "as fast as he could write," until the 1990s no quick recipe for doing so could be found. Even today, the methods of generation are somewhat cumbersome and difficult to implement. But it is easy to see how such a curious person as Benjamin Franklin— a scientist, inventor, statesman, printer, philosopher, musician, and economist— could create one of the most fascinating squares ever conceived. After Franklin's death, other magic-square researchers discovered new patterns in Franklin's number arrays.

That's the breathtaking aspect of magic squares. Armed with just a pencil and paper, you can discover new patterns in centuries-old magic squares. Each square is like a little treasure box waiting to be opened.

FINDING THE LOST SYMBOLS IN WASHINGTON, D.C.

Kryptos copyright © James Sanborn.

Decoding **Kryptos**   *By Greg Taylor*

A version of this chapter first appeared in Greg Taylor's Da Vinci in America. *It has been updated to reflect the appearance of* Kryptos *in* The Lost Symbol. *Taylor's new book is called* The Guide to Dan Brown's *The Lost Symbol.*

Fact or fiction? This simple question lies at the heart of Dan Brown's success. Though a writer of fiction, Dan Brown has taken to beginning his novels with a simple page titled "Fact," which then lists elements of the book that are allegedly based in reality. I say "allegedly" because much of the controversy driving Dan Brown's success has arisen out of the debate as to whether his "facts" mislead the reader into believing that much of the speculative history he presents is true. Case in point, Brown's statement at the beginning of *The Da Vinci Code* that "The Priory of Sion—a European secret society founded in 1099—is a real organization"; the consensus view on the Priory of Sion is actually that it is a modern hoax. Similarly, when Brown announces that "All descriptions of art-work, architecture, documents, and secret rituals in this novel are accurate," it's tempting to say that some of his "descriptions" veer somewhat from the strict definition of the word *fact*.

Much ink has been spilled discussing the controversial "facts" of *The Da Vinci Code*, so with the release of *The Lost Symbol*, it's worth taking a close look at Brown's claims in the new novel. It, too, features a "fact" page, which begins:

> *In 1991, a document was locked in the safe of the director of the CIA. The document is still there today. Its cryptic text includes references to an ancient portal and an unknown location underground. The document also contains the phrase "It's buried out there somewhere."*

It's certainly a statement that would pique a curious mind. What would the director of the Central Intelligence Agency be doing with a document referencing ancient portals and hidden underground locations locked in his safe? Various *Stargate SG-1* scenarios spring

James Sanborn. *Photo © James Sanborn.*

work to decorate the new building. The Agency requested submissions from artists interested in the $250,000 commission, outlining their desire that the pieces be not just pleasing to the eye, but also "indicative of the Central Intelligence Agency's work." In November 1988, Washington, D.C., artist James Sanborn was given the commission, based on his idea for a two-part sculpture to be known as *Kryptos* (Greek for "hidden"), which would sit in the main entrance and courtyard of the new building.

Sanborn was already well known for his ability to evoke a sense of mystery with his artwork, but *Kryptos* could well be regarded as his masterwork. Working with retired CIA cryptographer Ed Scheidt—described by the Agency's director as "The Wizard of Codes"—Sanborn devised a sculpture that would contain an enciphered puzzle, while itself presenting somewhat of a history of cryptography. The artwork begins beside the walkway from the parking deck, where granite "pages" emerge from the ground joined by copperplate, upon which are found early ciphers and International Morse. Also found in this area is a lodestone (naturally magnetized rock) along with a navigational compass rose.

into the imaginative mind, but the answer is a little more mundane than that unfortunately. The document that Dan Brown mentions actually references a sculpture that is just two decades old.

In the late 1980s construction work began on the New Headquarters Building (NHB) at the CIA's base in Langley, Virginia. Under Federal construction guidelines, a small percentage of the construction cost was earmarked for the commissioning of original art-

The best-known piece from *Kryptos* lies in the courtyard: an S-shaped copperplate screen "emerges" from a vertical piece of petrified wood and is surrounded by a bubbling pool of water. Almost 2,000 letters are cut out of the metal screen: The first half contains a table for deciphering and enciphering code, based on a method usually (mis)attributed to the sixteenth-century French cryptographer Blaise de Vigenère. The "Vigenère cipher" is a substitution cipher, which "shifts" each letter of the message to be encoded by various values (so a shift of 1 on the letter A would make it B, a shift of 2 on A would make it C, and so on), based on a keyword and the aforementioned table, generating what looks to be random text. The first two sections of *Kryptos* use this substitution table. The third employs a transposition cipher (moving the sequence of the letters around via a certain method, rather than shifting the value of the letters). The fourth section is unsolved, so the cipher method is unknown.

Despite sitting in the courtyard of perhaps the most well-known intelligence agency in the world, it would take more than seven years for one of the CIA's own to open a crack in the defenses of the enigmatic artwork. In February 1998, CIA physicist David Stein—working with just pencil and paper—happened on the first letter substitutions, and before too long he had cracked three of the four sections of *Kryptos*. However, his solutions were kept "in-house" at the Agency, so when California computer scientist Jim Gillogly announced just a year later that he too had cracked the first three sections (using a computer), he was at first believed to be the first person to do so. Only later was it announced that Stein had beaten him to the punch. (Additionally, the National Security Agency has now claimed that some of its analysts solved the first three sections in 1992.)

The first deciphered section of *Kryptos* is made up of a simple statement:

Between subtle shading and the absence of light lies the nuance of iqlusion.

Note the deliberate misspelling of "illusion"—Sanborn added a few of these "errors" into the sculpture's construction, just to make the deciphering even more difficult. The second section from *Kryptos* features a longer, curious message referring to magnetic fields and an unspecified object or location "buried out there somewhere":

It was totally invisible. How's that possible? They used the earth's magnetic field. The information was gathered and transmitted underground to an unknown location. Does Langley know about this? They should: it's buried out there somewhere. Who knows the exact location? Only WW. This was his last message: Thirty-eight degrees fifty-seven minutes six point five seconds North, seventy-seven degrees eight minutes forty-four seconds West. Layer two.

The third deciphered passage is equally tantalizing—it appears to be a paraphrase of the diary entry of Howard Carter on November 26, 1922—the day he discovered the tomb of the Pharaoh Tutankhamen (King Tut) at Luxor in Egypt. The message reads:

Slowly, desperately slowly, the remains of passage debris that encumbered the lower part of the doorway was removed. With trembling hands I made a tiny breach in the upper left-hand corner. And then, widening the hole a little, I inserted the candle and peered in. The hot air escaping from the chamber caused the flame to flicker, but presently details of the room within emerged from the mist. Can you see anything?

The final section though has stood the test of time. In the decade that has passed since Stein first solved the initial three sections, no one has made an impression on the remaining 97-character message. According to Sanborn's collaborator Ed Scheidt, there's a reason for that: "I saved the best for last."

The deciphered messages certainly have all the mystery of a Dan Brown novel. But how did Brown come to include *Kryptos* in *The Lost Symbol*? As *The Da Vinci Code* showed, the bestselling author has a keen interest in the field of cryptography and cipher techniques. Even before that novel though, Brown wrote about intelligence agencies and code-breaking in his 1998 book *Digital Fortress*. His fascination with the topic is perhaps based on his own experience growing up—he once recounted that during his childhood, his mathematician father would create treasure hunts involving ciphers and codes for Dan and his siblings to solve. It is likely that, through his lifelong fascination with cryptography, he was at sometime introduced to the subject of *Kryptos*—it is, after all, considered one of the world's great "unsolved codes."

One thing is certain though: *Kryptos* was planned as an element of *The Lost*

Symbol at least as far back as 2003. For on the dust jacket of the U.S. hardcover edition of *The Da Vinci Code* (published April 2003) can be found a number of ciphered messages. When originally found and deciphered by readers, these messages were ambiguous and confusing to say the least. However, the reason for their inclusion became obvious when Dan Brown announced a competition titled "Uncover the Code: The Secret is Hidden Right Before Your Eyes."

With the enticement of a trip to Paris for the winner, the Internet challenge began with these words: "Welcome fellow reader of *The Da Vinci Code*. Leonardo was a known trickster who liked to hide secrets in plain sight...Disguised on the jacket of *The Da Vinci Code*, numerous encrypted messages hint at the subject matter of Dan Brown's next Robert Langdon novel."

The first three questions of the challenge were a simple test of whether the participant had read *The Da Vinci Code;* once answered they gave way to the challenge proper. The first "real" question asked the reader to look on the back cover of Brown's best-seller and search for a coded reference written backwards. Keen observation—and a mirror—revealed a mysterious map reference:

37° 57' 6.5" North and 77° 8' 44" West. Before the Internet challenge was made available, those who had already found this code struck a dead end when they looked up the location. Why this was so became clear once the related question was asked in the WebQuest: *Q1. What enigmatic sculpture stands one degree North of the location indicated in the code?*

Adding on a degree to the latitude made more sense, as it pointed at the headquarters of the Central Intelligence Agency in Langley, Virginia—the "enigmatic sculpture" was therefore *Kryptos.*

Once "Kryptos" was entered as the answer on the website challenge, some background information on Sanborn's sculpture was given, including the deciphered second section ("They used the Earth's magnetic field..."). The website then asked for the concluding part of this text: *Q2. According to* Kryptos, *what are the initials of the person who "knows the exact location?"*

Anyone familiar with the *Kryptos* story would know this answer: a phrase in the deciphered second section from *Kryptos*, as mentioned above, is "Who knows the exact location? Only WW." The web competition offered no further comment on this answer, nor on *Kryptos* in general (though it's worth noting that the phrase "Only WW Knows" can be found discreetly placed upside down on the back cover of *The Da Vinci Code*). If we are to believe Sanborn's word, the "WW" referred to is the CIA director at the time of the sculpture's dedication, William Webster. The Agency, no doubt wary of an embarrassing message being encoded by the artist, had insisted that Sanborn give Webster an envelope containing the code and the message. Thus, "WW" should certainly know the solution—and this envelope is the document referred to on the "facts" page of *The Lost Symbol* (though Webster is no longer the CIA director). Others have cautioned against such an easy answer and continue to search for other options—some *Da Vinci Code* fans have even pointed out that WW turned upside down is MM, the initials of Mary Magdalene.

When asked about his interest in *Kryptos* during a TV interview, Brown replied that, apart from his attraction to codes and ciphers, it was because it "refers to the ancient mysteries." No doubt the sculpture's proximity to Washington, D.C.—an ideal location for a Dan Brown novel, with its esoteric architecture and "hidden history" featuring Freemasonry—helped. It's interesting to note that early reports said that

Kryptos had been designed in collaboration with a "prominent fiction writer." On the basis of this, rumors began to swirl that Brown was working closely with James Sanborn as part of the new book, but *Kryptos*'s creator was quick to dispute the claim. According to him, it was an idea he toyed with in the planning stage, but "I decided not to do it, why let someone else in on the secret?" In actual fact, Sanborn was said to be "deeply annoyed" at the prospect of *Kryptos* featuring in the sequel to *The Da Vinci Code*.

Nevertheless, mysteries remain. Despite its prominent place in the Da Vinci WebQuest, in *The Lost Symbol* the enigmatic sculpture ended up as a MacGuffin of sorts—a tangential "trivia item" that drove some parts of the plot forward, but ultimately turned out to be a red herring. Was this always Dan Brown's plan? Or was *Kryptos* originally a major part of the plot (remembering that *The Lost Symbol* was delivered four years late), but got "written out" when Sanborn announced his displeasure with its inclusion in the new book?

Another ongoing aspect to the mystery is whether "WW" really refers to William Webster. In the years leading up to the release of *The Lost Symbol* there was much speculation as to whether Dan Brown would announce his own candidate. Some of those included Mary Magdalene (WW upside down equals MM), anti-Masonic Presidential candidate William Wirt, and President Woodrow Wilson.

Ultimately though, Brown reiterated the William Webster identification—but he adds on that Nola Kaye (incidentally, a fictional name probably based on that of *Kryptos* expert Elonka Dunin) had "heard whispers once that it referred in fact to a man named William Whiston, a Royal Society theologian." It's curious that Dan Brown would include such a seemingly unrelated bit of trivia. Is it simply an offhand comment, does it refer to a previous plotline of *The Lost Symbol*, or is Brown pushing us to dig a little further into Whiston's background?

Doing so quickly refutes Brown's description: Whiston was a polymath, but was never allowed to join the Royal Society, perhaps due to his subscribing to the Christian heresy of Arianism. Dan Brown, however, could surely have made some mileage out of a portrait of Whiston, which shows him in the "John" pose (pointing the index finger) made famous in *The Da Vinci Code*.

However, the "Facts" page at the start of *The Lost Symbol*, describing the *Kryptos* message, is accurate. We could take issue with Brown's bending of the truth in saying it refers to "an ancient portal," when the third message actually describes making a hole through a wall into an ancient tomb (paraphrasing the discovery of the treasures of King Tutankhamen), though he could argue that point by definition alone. But the tantalizing points of the document referred to are essentially correct.

The interesting question is: Are these references to breathtaking discovery and buried underground locations actually pointing at a physical "treasure" that James Sanborn has put in place as the final solution to *Kryptos*? The artist says that even after the fourth section is deciphered, an additional riddle will need to be solved. Even beyond that, Sanborn's artwork is designed to be an everlasting abstract mystery. "I think all art should be subject to as many interpretations as possible," says Sanborn. "If there's nothing more to discover about it, then it's not a very interesting artwork.... They will be able to read what I wrote, but what I wrote is a mystery itself."

The Washington Monument by Elliott Teel. *Copyright © Elliott Teel.*

CHAPTER SIX
Conspiracy Theory

We conclude on an amusing note: Casaubon, the endearing protagonist of *Foucault's Pendulum*, is one of three clever editors who feed esoteric information into a computer program designed to find connections. Things soon get out of hand in one of the most intricate, diverting, and absorbing novels of the twentieth century.

Conspiracy Theory   *by Umberto Eco*

Rashly I volunteered to do some quick research. I soon regretted it. I found myself in a morass of books, in which it was difficult to distinguish historical fact from hermetic gossip, and reliable information from flights of fancy. Working like a machine for a week, I drew up a bewildering list of sects, lodges, conventicles. I occasionally shuddered on encountering familiar names I didn't expect to come upon in such company, and there were chronological coincidences that I felt were curious enough to be noted down. I showed this document to my two accomplices.

1645   London: Ashmole founds Invisible College, Rosicrucian in inspiration.

1660   From the Invisible College is born the Royal Society; and from the Royal Society, as everyone knows, the Masons.

1666   Paris: founding of the Académie Royal des Sciences.

1707   Birth of Claude-Louis de Saint-Germain, if he was really born.

1717   Creation of the Great Lodge in London.

1721   Anderson drafts the constitutions of English Masonry. Initiated in London, Peter the Great founds a lodge in Russia.

1730   Montesquieu, passing through London, is initiated.

1737   Ramsay asserts the Templar origin of Masonry. Origin of the Scottish rite, henceforth in conflict with the Great Lodge of London.

1738   Frederick, then crown prince of Prussia, is initiated. Later he is patron of Encyclopedists.

1740   Various lodges created in France around this year: Ecossais Fidèles of Toulouse. Souverain Conseil Sublime, Mère Loge Ecossaise du Grand Globe Français, Collège des Sublimes Princes du Royal Secret of Bordeaux, Cour des Souverains Commandeurs du Temple of Carcassonne, Philadelphes of Narbonne, Capitre des Rose-Croix of Montpellier, Sublimes Elus de la Vérité…

Elias Ashmole
by William Faithorne.
Line engraving, 1658.
© National Portrait Gallery, London.

1743 First public appearance of Comte de Saint-Germain. In Lyon, the degree of chevalier kadosch originates, its task being to vindicate Templars.

1753 Willermoz founds lodge of Parfaite Amitié.

1754 Martínez Pasqualis founds Temple of Elus Cohen (perhaps in 1760).

1756 Baron Von Hund founds Templar Strict Observance, inspired, some say, by Frederick II of Prussia. For the first time there is talk of the Unknown Superiors. Some insinuate that the Unknown Superiors are Frederick and Voltaire.

1758 Saint-Germain arrives in Paris and offers his services to the king as chemist, an expert in dyes. He spends time with Madame Pompadour.

1759 Presumed formation of Conseil des Empereurs d'Orient et d'Occident, which three years later is said to have drawn up the Constitutions et Règlement de Bordeaux, from which Ancient and Accepted Scottish rite probably originates (though this does not appear officially until 1801).

1760 Saint-Germain on ambiguous diplomatic mission in Holland. Forced to flee, arrested in London, released. Dom J. Pernety founds Illuminati of Avignon. Martínez Pasqualis founds Chevaliers Maçon Elus de l'Univers.

1762 Saint-Germain in Russia.

1763 Casanova meets Saint-Germain, as Surmont, in Belgium. Latter turns coin into gold. Willermoz founds Souverain Chapitre des Chevaliers de l'Aigle Noire Rose-Croix.

The Comte de Saint-Germain
St.-Germain is as great an enigma to us today as he was to his contemporaries. He was an outstanding scholar and linguist, who "spoke German, English, Italian, Portuguese, Spanish, French with a Piedmontese accent, Greek, Latin, Sanskrit, Arabic and Chinese with such fluency that in every land he visited he was accepted as a native." He painted, played several musical instruments and composed a short opera. He assisted Mesmer in developing the theory of mesmerism. "He was ambidextrous to such a degree that he could write the same article with both hands simultaneously. When the two pieces of paper were afterwards placed together with a light behind them, the writing on one sheet exactly covered, letter for letter, the writing on the other." He charmed both Casanova and Madame de Pompadour.

1768 Willermoz joins Pasqualis's Elus Cohen. Apocryphal publication in Jerusalem of *Les plus secrets mystères des haut grades de la maçonnerie devoilée, ou le vrai Rose-Croix:* it says that the lodge of the Rosicrucians is on Mount Heredon, sixty miles from Edinburgh. Pasqualis meets Louis Claude de Saint-Martin, later known as Le Philosophe Inconnu. Dom Pernety becomes librarian of king of Prussia.

Madame de Pompadour

1771 The Duc of Chartres, later known as Philippe-Egalité, becomes grand master of the Grand Orient (then, the Grand Orient of France) and tries to unify all the lodges. Scottish rite lodge resists.

1772 Pasqualis leaves for Santo Domingo, and Willermoz and Saint-Martin establish Tribunal Souverain, which becomes Grand Lodge Ecossaise.

1774 Saint-Martin retires, to become Philosophe Inconnu, and as delegate of Templar Strict Observance goes to negotiate with Willermoz. A Scottish Directory of the Province of Auvergne is born. From this will be born the Recitified Scottish rite.

1776 Saint-Germain, under the name Count Welldone, presents chemical plans to Frederick II. Société des Philathètes is born, to unite all hermeticists. Lodge of the Neuf Soeurs has as members Guillotin and Cabanis, Voltaire and Franklin. Adam Weishaupt founds Illuminati of Bavaria. According to some,

Voltaire

he is initiated by a Danish merchant, Kolmer, returning from Egypt, who is probably the mysterious Altotas, master of Cagliostro.

1778 Saint-Germain, in Berlin, meets Dom Pernety. Willermoz founds Ordre des Chevaliers Bienfaisants de la Cité Sainte. Templar Strict Observance and Grand Orient agree to accept the Recitfied Scottish rite.

1782 Great conference of all the initiatory lodges at Wilhelmsbad.

1783 Marquis Thomé founds the Swedenborg rite.

1784 Saint-Germain presumably dies while in the service of the landgrave of Hesse, for whom he is completing a factory for making dyes.

1785 Cagliostro founds Memphis rite, which later becomes the Ancient and Primitive rite of Memphis-Misraim; it increases the number of high degrees to ninety. Scandal of the Affair of the Diamond Necklace, orchestrated by Cagliostro. Dumas describes it as Masonic plot to discredit the monarchy. The Illuminati of Bavaria are suppressed, suspected of revolutionary plotting.

1786 Mirabeau is initiated by the Illuminati of Bavaria in Berlin. In London a Rosicrucian manifesto appears, attributed to Cagliostro. Mirabeau writes a letter to Cagliostro and to Lavater.

1787 There are about seven hundred lodges in France. Weishaupt publishes his Nachtag, which describes the structure of a secret organization in which each adherent knows only his immediate superior.

1789 French Revoluntion begins. Crisis in the French lodges.

1794 On 8 Vendémiaire, Deputy Grégoire presents to the Convention the project for a Conservatoire des Arts et Métiers. It is installed in Saint-Martin-des-Champs in 1799, by the Council of Five Hundred. The Duke of Brunswick urges lodges to dissolve because a poisonous subversive sect has now corrupted them all.

1798 Arrest of Cagliostro in Rome.

Copyright © George Stuart/Historical Figures Foundation.

The "Divine" Cagliostro
History suggests the Comte di Cagliostro was born in Sicily as Giuseppe Balsamo in 1743, but his friends believed him immortal; and to have taken part in the marriage feast of Cana. (He was accused by his enemies of being the Devil incarnate!)

He was the founder of the Egyptian Rite, advocated the inclusion of women into secret societies (since they had been admitted into the Ancient Mysteries) and initiated the Princesse de Lamballe.

1804 Announcement in Charleston of official foundation of Ancient and Accepted Scottish rite, with number of degrees increased to 33.

1824 Document from court of Vienna to French government denounces secret associations like the Absolutes, the Independents, the Alta Vendita Carbonara.

1835 The cabalist Oettinger claims to meet Saint-Germain in Paris.

1846 Viennese writer Franz Graffer publishes account of a meeting of his brother with Saint-Germain between 1788 and 1790. Saint-Germain received his visitor while leafing through a book by Paracelsus.

1865 Foundation of Societas Rosicruciana in Anglia (other sources give 1860, 1866, or 1867). Bulwer-Lytton, author of the Rosicrucian novel *Zanoni*, joins.

1868 Bakunin founds International Alliance of Socialist Democracy, inspired, some say, by the Illuminati of Bavaria.

1875 Elena Petrovna Blavatsky, with Henry Steel Olcott, founds the Theosophical Society. Her *Isis Unveiled* appears. Baron Spedalieri proclaims himself a member of Grand Lodge of the Solitary Brothers of the Mountain, Frater Illuminatus of the Ancient and Restored Order of the Manicheans and of the Martinists.

1877 Madame Blavatsky speaks of the theosophical role of Saint-Germain. Among his incarnations are Roger and Francis Bacon, Rosencreutz, Proclus, Saint Alban. Grand Orient of France eliminates invocation to the Great Architect of the Universe and proclaims absolute freedom of conscience. Breaks ties with Grand Lodge of England and becomes firmly secular and radical.

1879 Foundation of Societas Rosicruciana in the USA.

1880 Beginning of Saint-Yves d'Alveydre's activity. Leopold Engler reorganizes the Illuminati of Bavaria.

1884 Leo XIII, with the encyclical Humanum Genus, condemns Freemasonry. Catholics desert it; rationalists flock to it.

1888 Stanislas de Guaita founds Ordre Kabbalistique de la Rose-Croix. Hermetic Order of the Golden Dawn founded in England, with eleven degrees, from neophyte to ipissimus. Its imperator is McGregor Mathers, whose sister marries Bergson.

1890 Joseph Péladan, called Joséphin, leaves Guaita and founds the Rose-Croix Catholique du Temple et du Graal, proclaiming himself Sar Merodak. Conflict between Rosicrucians of Guaita's order and those of Péladan's is called the War of the Two Roses.

1891 Papus publishes his *Traité méthodique de science occulte.*

1898 Aleister Crowley initiated into Golden Dawn. Later forms Order of Thelema.

1907 From the Golden Dawn is born the Stella Matutina, which Yeats joins.

Aleister Crowley

1909 In the United States, H. Spencer Lewis "reawakens" the Anticus Mysticus Ordo Rosae

Crucis and in 1916, in a hotel, successfully transforms a piece of zinc into gold. Max Heindel founds the Rosicrucian Fellowship. At uncertain dates follow Lectorium Rosicrucianum, Frères Aînés de la Rose-Croix, Fraternitas Hermetica, Templum Rosae-Crucis.

1912 Annie Besant, disciple of Madame Blavatsky, founds, in London, Order of the Temple of the Rose-Cross.

1918 Thule Society is born in Germany.

1936 In France Le Grand Prieuré des Gaules is born. In the "Cahiers de la fraternité polaire," Enrico Contardi-Rhodio tells of a visit from Comte de Saint-Germain.

Annie Besant

FINDING THE LOST SYMBOLS IN WASHINGTON, D.C.

The Washington Monument: E Pluribus Unum

by Nicholas R. Mann

Nicholas R. Mann is the author of books on geomancy, mythology, the Celtic tradition, sacred geometry and, most recently, archaeoastronomy. His study on the system of numbers and geometric properties of the design of Washington are laid out in his book Sacred Geometry of Washington, D.C. *His book* Druid Magic *is described by the British Druid Order as "the single best work on the practice of modern Druidry in existence today." He received his BA with honors in ancient history and social anthropology at the University of London.*

There is a close connection between the creation of the Washington Monument and the L'Enfant Plan for Washington, D.C. Designed within sixty years of each other, both employ the ancient symbolic principles of sacred geometry; yet whereas there is no positive proof of the deliberate use of these skills in the L'Enfant Plan, the Washington Monument contains symbolic measures that are far too explicit to be anything other than deliberately employed.

Congress authorized the monument in 1800–01 following an initial resolution of 1783 to erect "an equestrian statue of George Washington." At that time the Senate did not approve the $200,000 appropriation, so nothing further was done about it, perhaps because of some unease over the nature of the proposed designs. A proposal made in 1799, for example, called for a marble pyramid, one hundred feet square at the base and this would have been entirely out of place. Other proposals included a "mausoleum" modeled on the original at Halicarnassus, considered one of the Seven Wonders of the Ancient World. This was a huge square platform surmounted by a colonnade and then a pyramid with a quadriga—horses and chariot with king inside—on top. Mausolus had been a Hellenistic despot claiming divine legitimation, so it seems probable that this proposal was considered inappropriate. However, the Freemasons later based their Washington, D.C., temple on this design.... L'Enfant himself had supported the original intent of

Left: Design by Robert Mills, 1846. Above: An 1852 projection of the completed monument.

Congress to erect an equestrian statue of the President. But by 1833 proposals were being made for an entirely different structure—an Egyptian-influenced obelisk. It is not entirely clear who thought of this first, but the architect Robert Mills is usually credited. His grand scheme of 1845 called for a six-hundred-foot shaft surrounded by a one-hundred-foot-high circular colonnade, upon which could go a chariot and horses. Perhaps the President was to have been placed dis-

creetly in the chariot, like a conquering emperor!

In 1833 a group of private citizens, many of them Freemasons, had formed the Washington National Monument Association and solicited subscriptions. By 1848, there were sufficient funds to begin construction of the obelisk. The cornerstone was laid on July 4 of that year, with the Grand Master of the Grand Lodge of the District, Benjamin B. French, presiding, attended by large numbers of Masons. The available funds proved to be insufficient for the colonnade and quadriga, so they were—fortunately—abandoned, but the obelisk went ahead. However, the engineers in charge of the project found that the site that had been chosen, which was located on the intersection of the axes through the White House and Capitol, was inadequate to provide a substantial foundation for this extremely heavy structure. So they moved the obelisk back from what was then the Potomac shore at the mouth of the Tiber to slightly higher and firmer ground. A smaller monument, commissioned by Thomas Jefferson and subsequently known as Jefferson Pier, was built to mark the actual point of intersection, but this is no longer in existence. The Mall was later realigned to the monument in a way that skewed it from the main east-west axis of the L'Enfant design.

The funds for this project continued to be limited, and after several long delays to construction, which included the Civil War, Congress finally stepped in and made an appropriation in 1876. The Washington Monument was finally dedicated in 1885 (Grand Master Benjamin B. French once again participated in the dedication ceremonies), and was opened to the public in 1888.

The Washington Monument is the tallest freestanding masonry structure in the world. Embedded in the internal walls of the shaft are ashlars—squared blocks—inscribed by the States of the

The two shades of stone used in the monument.

Union who sent them. Ashlars from other sources also appear. There are many from the various Masonic lodges around the nation. One was even sent by the Pope, but this disappeared in 1855; it was probably stolen and smashed. A suspicion that they was done by anti-Catholic Freemasons contributed to the circumstances that caused work on the monument to be delayed, but the greatest factor in the delay of the construction was the Civil War.

When work was resumed after the war, the stone used in construction was of a slightly different shade than that below, adding a discrete memorial of the effect of that conflict on the nation in the fabric of the monument.

The dimensions of the monument are as follows: The shaft has a height of

500.427 feet. The breadth of each side is 55.125 feet at the base, and 34.458 feet at the top. The pyramidion that forms the point of the obelisk has a height of 55 feet. This includes an aluminum pyramid on the tip that is 5.6 inches square and 8.9 inches high. The total height is therefore 555 feet 5.125 inches (although some sources say this should be 555 feet 6 inches), slightly more than ten times the breadth of the base.

The angle of slope of each face of the pyramidion is 72 degrees 36 seconds or 72.6 degrees. This is over half a degree more than the 72-degree angle present in the five-sided pentagon or pentacle. It seems curious that the 72.6-degree angle was chosen, when an angle of exactly 72

degrees would have placed the monument's pyramidion in the realm of the harmonious and "perfect" proportions of Golden Section geometry. Certainly the fives in the measures of the monument appear to relate it to the pentacle and Golden Section geometry.

Aspects of *gematria*, or numerological symbolism, inform the design—above all, the selection of the angle of 55 degrees between certain avenues. The pentacle is the symbol, *phi* is the proportion and 5 or 55 is the number representing the elements, the senses, and the matrix of animate life. Although there is no direct evidence that the Freemasons, who would certainly have been aware of such things, were involved with the

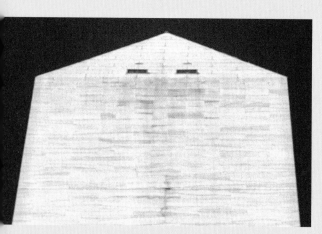

Above: The pyramidion on top of the shaft. Its "eyes" are windows through which visitors can look out over Washington. Right: The capstone, the very top of the Monument.

L'Enfant Plan, they were directly involved with commissioning the design of the Washington Monument. It seems very likely that the decision to make the monument 555 feet 5+ inches high was influenced by one or a number of the branches of Freemasonry that existed in the city at that time. These men would have had specific symbolism and meanings in mind that related to the number 5. Why the precise angle of the five-pointed pentacle or the pentalpha, 72 degrees, was not used for the crowning pyramidion seems therefore to pose us with something of a mystery.

Yet by considering the dimensions of the monument in inches we can solve the mystery. The obelisk's total height in inches is 6665.125+, which can be justifiably rounded up to 6666. The height of its pyramidion in inches is 660. The sides of its base in inches are 661.5. Then it is necessary to consider the angle of slope from the four corners of the base to the tip of the pyramidion. This is exactly 66 degrees 6 seconds, revealing the hidden number 666.

6666 and 666, like 66, 6, 660 and 60, are solar numbers and are connected with the circle and its six-fold geometry. In Islamic numerology, 66 is the numerical equivalent of Allah. In Judaism, the six-pointed star or hexagram is the "Seal of Solomon." It appears in every branch of Freemasonry. The associated 666 gains its notoriety in the West as the number of misused power and authority mentioned in the Book of Revelation; but more traditionally, 666 represents the solar principle. It is also a number of Christ. The sun, 666, shining from above, is the power that gives order to the chaos of earth. It is the masculine principle in action. Only if this power is misused will it lead to abuse. It was this unbalanced manifestation of 666 that the author of *Revelation* identified with the Antichrist or the "Beast." It is for this reason that 666 has come to be identified with concepts of the satanic, or extreme negativity, but this was emphatically not its original meaning.

L'Enfant appears to have favored six-fold geometry and 666 measures in his plan of the city around the White House. The monument to Washington was to be located 4 × 666 yards from the Capitol. An association of six—the number of the sun, action and authority—was most appropriate for the head of the hierarchy of government. And since towers have traditionally been associated with the sun, so the selection of an obelisk was also appropriate for this, the

Executive section of the city. In Islamic architecture, the minaret—"the place where light shines"—emphasizes the vertical, transcendent dimension of god. In ancient Egypt, the obelisk symbolized the rays of the sun.

The surprisingly exact manifestation of 6 or 666 in the various measures of the Washington Monument suggests these numbers were intentionally chosen by its architects and designers—men who either were themselves Freemasons or were influenced by this fraternity.

Evidently, the numbers were seen as having greater primary significance in the monument of a President—who was himself a Freemason—than did Golden Section proportions and their accompanying measures. The highest initiation a Freemason can achieve is defined by half of sixty-six, that is, the thirty-third degree. Furthermore, the lengths of the sides of the pyramidion, from the corners of the base to the tip are approximately 60 feet. This number, along with 666 and other six-based numbers, was seemingly selected to emphasize the six-fold symbology of the monument.

In fact the Washington Monument is a complex allegory in numbers. Created under the influence of the self-proclaimed inheritors of the ancient ar-

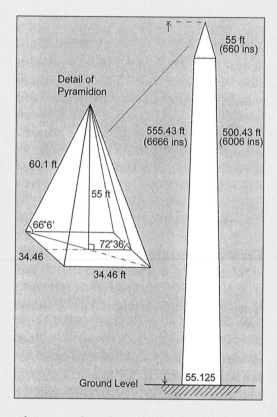

chitectural tradition, the Freemasons, it stands foursquare, the foundation of the temple. Any visible face of the pyramidion is a triangle, representing, among many things, the Trinity, or the dividers in the hand of the Supreme Architect. The Monument represents the single pillar of the nation, its lands and people, who are symbolized by the five-fold measures and the inscribed ashlars of each State in the shaft. It thus embodies in stone the national motto *E Pluribus Unum*, "From Many, One." Finally, the single pillar surmounted by the pyramidion has measures that fuse the numbers 5 and 555 with those of 6 and 666. 555 is the number of diversity and animate life. It is the earthly and lunar number. 666 is the authoritative and solar number of the head of the hierarchy, the President. It is particularly the number of the first, the founding President of the land.

666 and 1080

It is tempting to play with the numbers of the Washington Monument a little further. Some adjustment to the proportion seems to have been made to affect the numerical symbolism. For example, the height of the shaft is 500.427 feet. Why not exactly 500 feet or 6,000 inches?

If the object of the geometry was to reconcile 5 and 6, this would have seemed a good solution. However, to make the all important 66 degree 6 minute angles come out right, the designers needed that extra 0.427+ feet, or 5$\frac{1}{8}$ inches to add to the total height of the monument, and the pyramidion had to be precisely 55 feet in height, given a base of 34.458 feet. It is intriguing to note that the extra inches, when added to the length of a side at the base of the shaft, 55.125 feet, and the length of a side of the base of the pyramidion, 34.458 feet, add up to 90 feet.

$$55.125 + 34.458 + 0.427 = 90.01$$

Once again, these are strange numbers, as an even 55 feet for the base of the shaft would have yielded 660 inches. The intention of these minute adjustments is subtle however. For in the same way as the height of the Monument only reveals its meaning when given in inches, so the 90 feet measurement also reveals its full meaning when given in inches—1080. This number is equal in importance to 666 in *gematria*. It is the feminine, lunar and earthly number, the polar opposite of the number of the sun. 1080 is a number found in the angles of the pentacle, and it is highly appropriate to the measures of the shaft, whose ashlars represent the unity of the American nation. By adjusting the measures of the monument by a tenth of one percent, the Freemasons who designed the Washington Monument imbued it with a profoundly rich numerical symbolism.

Additional Places of Interest to Readers of
The Lost Symbol

Above: Washington, Jefferson and Madison wished to see a national garden in the capital, but it was not until 1820 that one was finally established by Congress. The rebuilt conservatory of the United States Botanic Garden opened in 2001.

Right: A mile and a half due north of the White House, Meridian Hill Park lies on the central meridian of the original District of Columbia, from the "home plate" southern boundary stone at Jones Point to the northern point of the diamond. Thirteen papyrus-lined cascading water basins descend the steep slope of the hill.

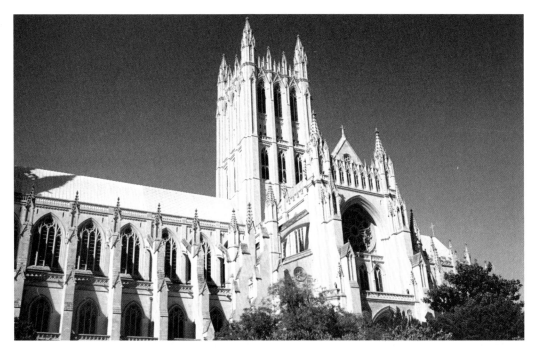

Robert Langdon and Katherine Solomon are re-captured at the National Cathedral (pictured above). Under construction for 83 years, it was completed in 1990. Its walls and flying buttresses are solid masonry, like the Gothic cathedrals of Europe.

Left: The Smithsonian Institution includes nearly a dozen museums on the Mall. It was established in 1846.

Right: At times the Smithsonian "Castle" and the Washington Monument conspire to give the capital of the republic the look of a medieval kingdom.

Notes, Sources, and Permissions

Unless otherwise credited, all photographs in the book were taken by Michael Bober and are copyright © 2009 by Michael D. Bober.

Library of Congress, Prints and Photographs Division: Chapter 2: LC-USZ62-31808, LC-USZC4-1090, LC-USZC4-771, LC-USZC4-11489, LC-USZ62-75795, LC-B8184-10205, LC-USZ62-104931, LC-USZ62-23939. Chapter 3: LC-USZC4-530. Chapter 6: LC-DIG-pga-03189, LC-USZC4-579, LC-H824-T-M04-045. Library of Congress, Maps Division. Chapter 3: g3850 ct001865, g3851s cw0674000.

Chapter One

Kleinknecht quote ("Hidden in Plain Sight") is from his Introduction to *The Secret Architecture of Our Nation's Capital* by David Ovason.

Manly Hall quote is from his book *The Secret Teachings of All Ages.*

"Speculative Masonry" by Jasper Ridley is excerpted from his chapter three, entitled "The Seventeenth Century" of *The Freemasons,* Copyright © 1999 by Jasper Ridley, published by Arcade Publishing, New York, NY. Footnotes to this excerpt are as follows:

1. Knoop and Jones, *Genesis of Freemasonry,* 130-1.
2. Ibid. 97; Lane, 27, 31.
3. Matt. xvi.18.
4. Geneva Bible, notes to I Sam.xxvi.9.
5. 2 Chron., chaps. ii-viii.
6. Knoop and Jones, *Genesis of Freemasonry,* 90.
7. Piatigorsky, 46-48, 59, 61, 63, 92-102.
8. White, *Issac Newton,* 158-162; Peters, "Sir Issac Newton and the 'The Oldest Catholic Religion' "; Peters, "Sir Issac Newton and the Holy Flame" (*AQC,* c.192-6; ci.207-13).
9. *Early Masonic Pamphlets,* 30, 79.

10. Knoop and Jones, *Genesis of Freemasonry,* 92.
11. Jackson, "Rosicrusianism and its Effect on Craft Masonry" (*AQC,* xcvii.124).
12. Ibid.; Hamill and Gilbert, *Freemasonry: A Celebration of the Craft,* 20.
13. Hamill and Gilbert, *Freemasonry: A Celebration of the Craft,* 254; Knoop and Jones, *Genesis of Freemasonry,* 132; Rogers, "The Lodge of Elias Ashmole" (*AQC,* lxv.38).
14. Plot, *The Natural History of Stafford-shire,* 316; *Early Masonic Pamphlets,* 31.
15. Williamson and Baigent, "Sir Christopher Wren and Freemasonry: New Evidence" (*AQC,* cix.188-90).
16. Castells, *English Freemasonry in the Period of Transition,* 36; Knoop and Jones, *Genesis of Freemasonry,* 144.
17. For the proceedings against the Templars (*AQC,* xx.47-70, 112-42, 269-342).
18. Barruel, *Mémoires pour server à l'histoire du Jacobisme,* ii.376.
19. For the many theories of the story of the Knights Templars in Scotland, see especially Robinson, *Born in Blood,* passim.

"Sufi Origins" by Robert Graves is excerpted from his Introduction to *The Sufis* by Idries Shah copyright c 1964 by Robert Graves, published by Jonathan Cape, London, England. Reprinted by permission of Carcanet Press.

"The Lost Word" by Gerard de Nerval is excerpted from *Journey to the Orient,* originally published in French in 1851, translated by Nicholas Glass and published by NYU Press in 1972. This chapter was originally titled "Makbenash" and is copyright © NYU Press.

"As Above, So Below," is excerpted from *The Secret Teachings of All Ages.*

"Symbolic Masonry" is excerpted from John J. Robinson's *Born in Blood*, copyright © John J. Robinson 1989, published by M. Evans & Co.

"The Wayfarer" is excerpted from *A Pilgrim's Path* by John J. Robinson, copyright © John J. Robinson, 1993 and published by M. Evans & Company.

"The Knights Templar and the Secret of the Scroll" is copyright © 2009 by John White. Footnotes to this extract are:

1. W. L. Tucker, "Royal Arch Masonry," *Royal Arch Mason* (spring 2001, p. CT-5).
2. Thomas C. Berry, letter to editor, *Royal Arch Mason* (summer 2001, p. 167).

The Capitol

Text concerning *The Apotheosis of Washington*, National Statuary Hall, and the Statue of Freedom are from the Office of the Architect of the Capitol.

Chapter Two

"The Invisible College" is excerpted from *The Rosicrucian Enlightenment* by Frances Yates copyright ©1972 by Frances A. Yates and reprinted by permission of Taylor & Francis.

"Masonic Civility During the Revolutionary War" is excerpted from *The Temple and the Lodge* by Michael Baigent and Richard Leigh, copyright © 1991 by Michael Baigent and Richard Leigh and reprinted by permission of Arcade Publishing, New York, NY.

"The Great Seal of the United States" is excerpted from © by Joseph Campbell & Bill Moyers, copyright © 1988 by Apostrophe S Productions, Inc., and Bill Moyers and Alfred Van der Marck Editions, Inc., for itself and the estate of Joseph Campbell. Used by permission of Doubleday, a division of Random House, Inc.

Chapter Three

"The Great Dinner" and "Pierre L'Enfant Designs the Federal City" are both copyright © 2009 by Michael D. Bober.

"Pierre L'Enfant and the Sacred Geometry of Washington, D.C." is reprinted from *The Sacred Geometry of Washington, D.C.* by Nicholas R. Mann copyright © 2006 by Nicholas R. Mann and reprinted by permission of Green Magic.

Kryptos
Kryptos originally appeared in *Da Vinci in America* copyright © 2004 by Greg Taylor. Additional material has been added copyright © 2009 also by Greg Taylor. Reprinted by permission of Daily Grail Publishing, Brisbane, Australia.

Chapter Six

"Conspiracy Theory" by Umberto Eco is excerpted from *Foucault's Pendulum*, translated by William Weaver, copyright © 1988 by Gruppo Editoriale Fabbri Bompiani, Sonzog Etas S.p.A., Milano. English translation copyright © 1989 by Harcourt, Inc., reprinted by permission of Harcourt, Inc.

The Washington Monument

"The Washington Monument: *E Pluribus Unum*" is reprinted from *The Sacred Geometry of Washington*, D.C. by Nicholas R. Mann copyright © 2006 by Nicholas R. Mann and reprinted by permission of Green Magic.

About the Editors

John Weber is the editor of *The Tao of Bada Bing* and *The World According to Rummy*.

Patrick Huyghe is the editor and publisher of *The Anomalist*.

Michael Bober is a filmmaker, producer of *Favorite Son: Alexander Hamilton* and *The Making of Mary Silliman's War.*